HOLOCAUST:

GERMAN HISTORY AND OUR HALF-JEWISH FAMILY

Thomas Paul Bernstein

"This exquisite, deeply disturbing memoir of growing up half-Jewish in the Third Reich presents a beautifully drawn portrait of a loving family forced to endure unforgivable trauma and loss. Written by a distinguished scholar with the assistance of his older sister, it traces the development of antisemitism in Germany thus providing gripping – horrific – details of how Nazi policies decimated one family. The two parents – soulmates who loved each other and their children – could be any of us. To watch as their world crumbled, and view the harmful toll the Nazis inflicted on the entire family, is painful beyond words but is a necessary reminder of the harm hatred and prejudice can do. Most importantly, the book resonates with the authors' love for their extraordinary parents and is a striking tribute to the resilience of the human soul."

— Kristen Renwick Monroe, Chancellor's Distinguished Professor of Political Science at UC Irvine and the founding Director of the UCI Ethics Center

"Bernstein offers an exceedingly rare description and analysis of how some Jews were able to survive in Germany during the Nazi reign. The most moving chapters are those that describe what it was like to live in Germany during the Nazi years and why his parents didn't try to emigrate before it was too late. The writing in this book is direct, clear, and elegant in its simplicity."

— Irving Leonard Markovitz, Professor Emeritus of Political Science, Queens College and the Graduate Center of CUNY

"This book appeals both to our emotions as well as our intellect. It is a moving personal memoir and family history as well as a compelling history of German-Jewish relations in the nineteenth and twentieth centuries, the emergence and irrationality of antisemitism, and the nightmare that followed.

German Fascism, we see, did not start with Auschwitz and the gas chambers, nor did it start with the so-called *Kristallnacht,* now usually referred to as November pogroms. It started, much earlier, with words and poisoning language, uttered not only by politicians and party propagandists but also by renowned intellectuals and artists, ostracizing and demonizing a group of people, many of whom, like Thomas Bernstein's father, a veteran of WW I, considered themselves German at heart. As a historian and academic of political science, Bernstein offers many a detail that will be new information even for those familiar with the dark, twentieth-century German history. It is also enlightening regarding present-day politics, as we witness Western democracies under threat by autocratic and populist leaders and movements. "Beware of the Beginnings", and "Never Again", are the clear messages to the reader.

I only wish Prof. Bernstein's father had known that his small son, who just started school when he was murdered in Auschwitz, would grow to become a successful academic and write this moving family memoir in the distant future!"

— Dr. Phil. Regula Venske,
President emerita of German PEN

"This moving memoir tells the Holocaust experiences of a family in which the father was Jewish, but the wife was not. So Tom Bernstein and his older sister Barbara were only half-Jewish, both born after Hitler came to power. Their parents thought that the father's status as a veteran and the mother not being Jewish would protect them. Much of the memoir tells how mistaken that hope was, with both parents losing jobs, having to move several times, entering into a divorce to try to protect the children, and the father eventually forced into a ghetto and then transported to Auschwitz, where he was murdered. But this is also an inspiring account of determination to survive and a mother's efforts to rely on networks of friends to help look after her children, as the family repeatedly escaped arrest threats and temporary separations. Tom was brought to America after the war to live with a Cornell professor who had forged a bond with his father in Germany in the 1920s, and he went on to become a very successful specialist on Chinese politics, teaching at both Yale and then Columbia. As a close friend of Tom's for many years, I was stunned to learn how disrupted and chaotic his early life had been, so different from my own, and this memoir serves as an inspiring example of Tom's ability to overcome unbelievably awful early life experiences and build a successful life."

— Martin K. Whyte, John Zwaanstra Professor of
International Studies and Sociology, Harvard University

HOLOCAUST: GERMAN HISTORY AND OUR HALF-JEWISH FAMILY

Thomas Paul Bernstein

With contributions by Barbara J. R. Bernstein

CHERRY ORCHARD BOOKS

2024

Library of Congress Cataloging-in-Publication Data
Names: Bernstein, Thomas P., author. | Bernstein, Barbara J. R., 1935- author.
Title: Holocaust : German history and our half-Jewish family / Thomas P. Bernstein, with contributions by Barbara J.R. Bernstein.
Other titles: German history and our half-Jewish family
Description: Boston : Cherry Orchard Books, 2024. | Includes bibliographical references.
Identifiers: LCCN 2024044119 (print) | LCCN 2024044120 (ebook) | ISBN 9798887196183 (hardback) | ISBN 9798887196190 (paperback) | ISBN 9798887196206 (adobe pdf) | ISBN 9798887196213 (epub)
Subjects: LCSH: Holocaust survivors--Biography. | Mischlinge (Nuremberg Laws of 1935) | Moosdorf, Johanna. | Bernstein, Barbara J. R., 1935- | Bernstein, Thomas P. | Bernstein, Paul, 1897-1944?--Family. | Children of interfaith marriage--Germany--Biography. | Holocaust, Jewish (1939-1945)--Personal narratives. | Jews--Germany--History--1933-1945. | Holocaust, Jewish (1939-1945)--Germany. | Bernstein family.
Classification: LCC DS134.4 .B476 2024 (print) | LCC DS134.4 (ebook) | DDC 940.53/180922--dc23/eng/20241023

LC record available at https://lccn.loc.gov/2024044119
LC ebook record available at https://lccn.loc.gov/2024044120

ISBN 9798887196183 hardback
ISBN 9798887196190 paperback
ISBN 9798887196206 ebook PDF
ISBN 9798887196213 epub

Book design by Kryon Publishing Services
Cover design by Ivan Grave

Published by Cherry Orchard Books, an imprint of Academic Studies Press
1007 Chestnut Street
Newton, MA 02464
press@academicstudiespress.com
www.academicstudiespress.com

In memory of our parents

This history depicts the lives of our family from the 1890s into the twenty-first century. Its centerpiece is our experiences during the Nazi regime. Our father, Paul Bernstein, was Jewish; his wife, Johanna Moosdorf, was not. A wounded and decorated WWI veteran, Paul was for some time exempted from deportation, but in the end was murdered in Auschwitz. We, Paul's and Johanna's two half-Jewish children, Barbara and Thomas, born in 1935 and 1937, were in some danger during the war, but survived in part because Nazi policy distinguished between full- and half-Jews and because of our mother's heroic efforts to keep us safe. For this reason, and because of her deep anxieties about her husband, Johanna was under enormous stress, which after liberation led to a collapse and five months of hospitalization. Since the war, we have lived with the legacies of our family's tragedy. In order to provide context and explanations, this family story is deeply embedded in extensive academic and primary research on the Holocaust and modern Germany.

Contents

Acknowledgments

I thank the following individuals for providing material for this history: Barbara Bernstein, Amelie Döge, Karl Moosdorf, Thomas F. Remington, and Regula Venske. I also thank Steven M. Goldstein, Gunther Heilbrunn, Irving L. Markovitz, Andrew J. Nathan, Katherine Ragsdale, Carl Riskin, and Wang Feng for reading earlier versions of the manuscript and providing brief comments. Special thanks go to Kristen R. Monroe, Regula Venske and Martin K. Whyte for their detailed comments, as well as to Laura Long for her detailed comments and many editorial suggestions.

I am very grateful to my two daughters, Anya Bernstein Bassett and Maia Bernstein, born in 1968 and 1974, who always supported and encouraged me to undertake this project. Both are quite aware of their grandfather's fate and its impact on me. I wrote this book for them. Anya and her husband, Jonathan Bassett, have two children, Benjamin Paul and Sarah Bassett, born in 1997 and 2000, know about their great-grandfather, but the details of what happened are much more remote to them. Anya also went over the MS with a fine toothcomb, and I thank her most warmly.

I am most grateful to my wife, Dorothy J. Solinger, who read all the drafts, made extensive substantive comments, and edited the manuscript, greatly improving its readability. She brought enthusiasm, comfort, and encouragement to this project, all indispensable to its completion.

Sincere thanks to Alessandra Anzani, Stuart Allen, Kira Nemirovsky, and Ilya Nikolaev of Academic Studies Press for their hard work bringing this project to fruition.

Any remaining mistakes are entirely mine.

Permissions

Festiner, John. *Paul Celan: Poet, Survivor, Jew*. New Haven: Yale University Press, 1995. Permission by Estate.

Geheran, Michael. *Comrade Betrayed: Jewish WWI Veterans under Hitler*. Ithaca: Cornell University Press, 2020.

Levitsky, Steven, and Daniel Ziblatt. *How Democracies Die*. New York: Penguin Random House Press, 2018. Authors' permission.

Levitsky, Steven, and Daniel Ziblatt. *Tyranny of the Majority: Why America Reached the Breaking Point*. New York: Penguin Random House Press, 2023. Authors' permission.

Remington, Thomas F. *The Returns to Power: A Political Theory of Inequality*. Oxford: Oxford University Press, 2023. Author's permission.

Abbreviations

GOP—Republican Party

DDR—Deutsche Demokratische Republik (German Democratic Republic, East Germany)

KPD—Komunistische Partei Deutschlands (German Communist Party)

MAGA—Make America Great Again.

NSDAP—Nationalsozialistische Deutsche Arbeiterpartei (National Socialist German Workers Party, Nazis)

OKW—Oberkommando der Wehrmacht (Supreme Command of the Armed Forces)

SED—Sozialistische Einheits Partei Deutschlands (Socialist Unity Party)

SA—Sturmabteilung (Storm Trooper Detachment)

SS—Schutzstaffel (Protective Echelon)

VRA—Voting Rights Act

Wannsee—Die Wansee Konferenz vom 20. January 1942

Note on Sources

This history is based on many conversations with our mother, Johanna Moosdorf (1911–2000), and a lengthy letter she wrote to Barbara and me in 1966, which contains rich detail about her husband's early life, his personality, his work in adult education, and political activities prior to the Nazi takeover in 1933. Johanna was a German novelist and poet, and several of her books dealt with the Nazi period. Her novel *Jahrhundertträume* (Dreams of the century, 1989) is about the relations between Jews and Germans. Much of it is a fictionalized depiction of her marriage to our father, Paul Bernstein, using pseudonyms. It contains much information about her harrowing experiences during the Nazi period. Other novels dealt with the legacy of the Nazi past. For example, *Nebenan* (Next door), translated, published, and reviewed in the US in 1964, portrays an SS doctor who after the war concealed his experiments on concentration camp inmates. *Die Andermanns* (1969) is about generational conflicts over Germany's past.

My sister, Barbara, who was born in 1935 and is two years older than me, remembers more than I do about our past, especially about our father. She wrote lengthy letters to me about her experiences—for instance, about hurtful antisemitic incidents that occurred in elementary school. Her memories are enhanced by decades of mother-daughter conversations. Her contributions were extremely valuable.

A German writer and literary scholar, Regula Venske, a close friend of our mother's, provided both information and insights. In *Dreams of the Century*, Johanna thanked Regula for her "encouragement and comfort and making it easier to remember" the past (301). Regula has been part of the German effort to keep memories of the Holocaust alive. She has written penetrating articles, book chapters, and comments about Johanna's writings, some appended to her books (Venske).

An American woman, Alice Hanson Cook, met our father in the late 1920s while studying in Germany. They shared interests in adult education and trade unions. After WWII she returned to occupied Germany, and in 1952, she and her son, Philip, invited me to live with them in the

United States. Her autobiography *A Lifetime of Labor* (1998) contains many details and acute observations important to this history.

Karl Moosdorf, a grandson of Johanna's brother, Willi, provided information about his side of the family and about Habertshof, a boarding school for adult education where Paul taught from 1930 to 1932. He also provided me with correspondence written by Johanna and a genealogy of the Moosdorfs.

I owe a huge debt to a Berlin woman, Amelie Döge, who has long been intensively engaged in researching the fate of Germany's murdered Jews. Amelie located relevant archives where I discovered key documents. She also found old newspapers, publications by Jewish community groups, and address books that were proved very useful. Most importantly, she helped me acquire political articles that our father wrote between 1929 and 1932.

I incorporated much material on German history and the Holocaust from the academic literature and from primary sources in order to provide explanations and context, and to make inferences about gaps in the story. Fritz Stern's *Five Germanys That I Have Known* combines family history with trenchant historical analysis. It is was a model for the kind of task that I set for myself. Chapter 3 "From Persecution to Genocide" is intended to set the stage for Chapters 4 and 5 about our family during the Nazi years. It is selective in its focus on matters of salience to the family, such as the fate of WWI veterans, since our father was one of them, and of Jews married to gentiles, which was the case with our parents. I use passages from Adolf Hitler's *Mein Kampf* (My Struggle) to highlight his virulent antisemitism and passages from speeches by Reichsführer-SS, Heinrich Himmler, who implemented the Holocaust. I also used documents from German archives, such as the property declarations that German Jews had to fill out prior to their deportation. The Epilogue analyzes how postwar Germany sought to prevent the rise of another dictator with a comparison of how the US has responded to the threat of Donald Trump.

CHAPTER 1

German Antisemitism

The Nineteenth Century

Our family lived in a society in which at least four types of antisemitic beliefs and feelings freely circulated. One was belief in the centuries-old derogatory stereotypes about Jews, such as their greed for money. Another was hostility towards the emancipation of Jewry and its integration into German institutions and society. A third was hostility to Jewish refugees escaping from tsarist pogroms. The fourth was the notion that Jews were not simply members of a religion but a separate and alien race that posed an existential threat to the gentile world.

Historical circumstances fed these prejudices. First, the strains, stresses, and dislocations of rapid modernization in the nineteenth century were one source of antisemitism. As Germany grappled with these pressures, acrimonious and contentious debates arose between the competing ideologies of reactionaries, conservatives, liberals, and leftist radicals about politics, ideology, society, culture, and the economy. A major question centered on how and when the longstanding division of Germany into separate states could be overcome. Under Otto von Bismarck's leadership, Prussia, the largest German state, went to war with the Austro-Hungarian Empire in 1866 and with France in 1870–71. During the latter conflict imperial Germany was founded and the country unified as a federal state (Ozment, chapter 8).

Second, the emancipation of Jewry in Western Europe in the late eighteenth and nineteenth centuries ended the prohibitions and restrictions long imposed on Jewish communities. German Jews were now able to enter public life, the civil service, the professions and the cultural sphere, and to become entrepreneurs. Jews made up only 1.24% of the population, but their achievements and wealth were disproportionate. Many enrolled in secondary schools and universities. By the 1860s, 17% of the country's bankers were Jewish, as were 16% of lawyers, and 10% of physicians (ibid, 277). Some Jews, such as Karl Marx, whose socioeconomic theories on class struggle, capitalism, and revolution had an immense impact worldwide. So did Sigmund Freud's theory of psychoanalysis and Albert Einstein's theory of relativity. Others became leaders of socialist and liberal parties, and still others, famous composers, novelists, and painters.

Jews made up 10% of Germany's physicians. Fritz Stern's family was a notable example of their high status:

> My four great-grandfathers, my two grandfathers, and my father all were physicians, and their successes and setbacks were characteristic of their class—increasingly prosperous until at least 1914, and professionally innovative and eminent, with a very distinct ethos (Stern, 16–17).

In 1938 the family fled to the United States and Stern became a distinguished professor of German history at Columbia University. He frequently returned to Germany and as an honored guest was invited to speak to the Bundestag (National Parliament).

The success of Jews aroused resentment, envy, and fears of their growing influence and power. Antisemitism was widespread among conservatives and the military, many of whom thought of them as alien and un-German. They were largely excluded from the officer corps and had difficulty entering the civil service (chapter 1).

Third, in the later decades of the nineteenth century, antisemitic sentiments were aroused by the influx of Russian and Polish Jews who migrated to Germany and elsewhere to escape intensified persecution in Tsarist Russia. *The Protocols of the Elders of Zion,* concocted by the tsarist secret police, accused Jewry of a scheme to dominate the world, just one example of the propaganda that sought to provoke anti-Jewish violence. Numerous pogroms, violent assaults on Jewish communities, prompted the exodus. The *Protocols* became a staple of antisemitic agitation.

Jewish refugees settled in Berlin and in other cities. Many continued to adhere to the Orthodox branch of Judaism and its fundamentalist precepts and practices. Germans often disdained these migrants, seeing them as alien "others." A good many German Jews shared these views and supported the

Reform movement that sought to modernize Judaism and promote assimilation to the dominant culture.

Fourth, antisemitic intellectuals regarded Jews as a separate, inferior race and not simply as members of a religion. This view was heightened by then popular social Darwinist theories about the survival of the fittest. These intellectuals claimed that Aryans, an Indo-European people "believed to have migrated west . . . from India . . . during the second millennium B.C. was the purest and strongest. . . . Many Germans believed it to be the Nordic Aryan race, or themselves" (196). Richard Wagner, the celebrated composer of hugely popular Teutonic operas, shared such beliefs. His son-in-law, Houston Stuart Chamberlain, an antisemitic theorist, "made the Wagner's home base a mill for such biological/racist thinking":

> How ominous such scholarly speculations were was confirmed decades later, when Adolf Hitler, then a struggling Nazi Party leader who had read Chamberlain's book, met the old man on his deathbed and kissed his hands. Although no one could have imagined it at the time, that kiss began the long descent of German racism into Jewish persecution and genocide" (196–7).

But, despite anti-Jewish agitation and occasional acts of violence, Jewish communities continued to thrive in Germany. "Hatred of Jews was slow to become focused and developed into a systematic campaign" (277). The notorious Dreyfus affair in France had no counterpart in Germany.

Adolf Hitler's Virulent Hatreds

Hitler's animus crystallized during his years in Vienna, 1908–1913, then the capital of the Austro-Hungarian Empire, a multinational state inhabited by Germans, Czechs, Jews, and other ethnic groups. The country was riven by demands for independence, as in the case of the Czechs, and for separation by Germans who longed for incorporation into the German Reich.

Vienna was a cosmopolitan city, famous for its cultural and intellectual achievements and its exciting and vibrant life. Hitler, however, did not do well there. An aspiring painter, he applied to study at the prestigious Academy of Fine Arts, but was rejected, a bitter disappointment. He spent these years as a lonely, aimless individual, drifting from to job to job. He earned little and he had to take refuge in a men's shelter.

Hitler's dismal life left him disoriented, full of anger and resentment, and in search of someone to blame for his plight. He settled on the Jews. At the time, Vienna was home to about two hundred thousand Orthodox and assimilated Jews, amounting to about 10% of the city's population. Many had prospered, taking advantage of the city's abundant opportunities, and some occupied important positions in social hierarchies and government. Vienna also harbored numerous vitriolic Jew-haters, one of whom was Vienna's mayor. Antisemites freely disseminated their scurrilous opinions (Fest, chapters 1–3). Tom Stoppard's play *Leopoldstadt* (2020) vividly portrays the lives of Viennese upper-class Jews and their fate after Nazi Germany annexed Austria in 1938.

In *Mein Kampf* the future Führer depicts his conversion to fanatical antisemitism: He wrote that he suddenly ran across an apparition in a long caftan and black locks. "My first thought was to ask, is this also a Jew?" He wondered why this man was so different from the Jews he had known in Linz, his hometown. A second question popped into his mind: "is this also a German?" (59). He began to buy antisemitic pamphlets and embarked on a tortuous mission to find out all he could about Jews, ending up utterly horrified by what he learned about their goals and behavior. He came to detest them as dirty, unmanly, greedy, glib, shameless, underhanded, and always ready to lie, deceive, and mislead:

> Was there any form of filth or profligacy, particularly in cultural life, without at least one Jew involved in it? If you cut even cautiously into such an abscess, you found, like a maggot in a rotting body, often dazzled by the sudden light—a kike.

And he reviled them as sexual predators, having had a

> nightmarish vision of the seduction of hundreds and thousands of girls by repulsive, bandy-legged Jew bastards. . . . With satanic joy, the black-haired Jewish youth looks for the unsuspecting girl whom he defiles with his blood, thus stealing from her people (quoted in Fest 1974, 39–40).

In Vienna Hitler was only a passive observer and not an active participant in anti-Jewish activities. He also did not formulate a coherent policy of how to combat the deadly Jewish "menace." As he learned more, he agreed with the thesis of the "Protocols of the Elders of Zion" that Jews were a separate race that posed an existential threat to gentile mankind. He became convinced that Jews were busily scheming to infiltrate, subvert, and undermine gentile political, economic, social educational and cultural institutions so as to erode their capacity to resist Jewish entrenchment in these institutions. For instance, he claimed that socialist parties portrayed themselves as the champions of the proletariat, which was suffering under capitalist exploitation. But these parties were dominated by "Jewish Marxism" and instead of genuinely fighting for their interests, they deceived workers only to gain influence and power over them. Hitler adds that the workers needed to be rescued (*Mein Kampf*, 69). After WWI, the Nazi Party included "worker" in its title.

> What set Hitler apart was his manic obsession with Jews as a world-wide conspiracy. The Jew had 75% of the world's capital and dominated Marxist parties. He undermined governments, bastardized races, glorified fratricide, fomented civil war, justified baseness, and poisoned nobility: the wirepuller of the destinies of mankind (Ozment, 101).

Hitler's Military Service and Turn to Politics

In 1913, Hitler fled to Munich, Germany, to avoid being drafted into the Austrian army. But when WWI broke out, he enthusiastically petitioned the Bavarian government to allow him to enlist, and his request was granted. He served in Belgium and France during the four years of war. As a soldier, he found a cause in which he fervently believed and abandoned his former life of despair and aimlessness. Hitler was a disciplined and obedient soldier whom superiors praised for invariably carrying out his duties. Thomas Weber's *Hitler's First War* notes that he "remained steadfast in his support for the war," even as many other soldiers eventually longed for peace (69).

Weber debunks Nazi propaganda that extolled Hitler's exceptional bravery because he was attached to a regimental headquarters that usually kept him away from the bloody trenches. Prior to 1933, anti-Nazi researchers found that a good many ordinary soldiers were decorated because of their personal relations with officers. These scholars surmised that Hitler's award of two Iron Crosses might also have the result of his closeness to officers (94–104). However, he was wounded twice, once in 1916 and once in October 1918 when he was sent back to Germany having been temporarily blinded in a British gas attack.

The war greatly strengthened Hitler's far-right beliefs. He desperately wanted Germany to win, since, he imagined, this would lead to the emergence of a purified society that rejected "cosmopolitan ideas and degenerate ways" thereby fostering the solidarity needed to heal the country's "fractured and divided state" (Weber, 74).

Germany's defeat in November 1918 was a shattering blow. He wrote that he burst into tears when he heard of the Armistice and "resolved to become a politician" to save his adopted fatherland. For more than a year he stayed with his regiment, which ordered him to report on the many small political groups that had sprung up in Munich. Some consisted of rightwing radicals who bitterly opposed the "Bavarian Socialist Republic" founded just after the war and that took Lenin's Bolshevik Revolution as a model. Though it was crushed in short order, it became a vivid symbol for the far right to legitimate its claim to be a bulwark against communism. Many Germans viewed Bolshevism as essentially Jewish, but veterans, including some who had served in Hitler's regiment, were more or less exempt from the hatred directed at non-veterans, a point of significance discussed in Chapter 3.

In the fall of 1919, Hitler attended a meeting of the tiny German Workers' Party whose members were thrilled by his ability to speak persuasively to them. He left the military and in short order was elected leader of the party (Weber, 257–8), now known as the National Socialist Workers Party. His new-found talent as an electrifying orator greatly helped him to rise to power and during the Nazi regime.

In *Mein Kampf*, Hitler wrote that

> Jews dominate Russia but will destroy it. Fate has chosen Germany to be a witness to a catastrophe, the most powerful testimony to the correctness of folkish race theory (743).

He blamed Jews and their lackeys for Germany's defeat in 1918, for "stabbing the army in the back" (*Dolchstoss*) even while pretending to have fought as patriotic Germans. If, he argued,

> 12,000 of these scoundrels had been done away with at the appropriate time, perhaps a million of proper Germans, valuable for the future, could have been saved. . . . While bourgeois *Staatskunst* (statecraft) didn't hesitate to send millions to die in battle, it regards 10,000–12,000 of these [Jewish] traitors, fraudsters, usurers, and deceivers as an untouchable, sacred treasure (772).

Hitler called for sustained efforts to revive the German martial spirit and the heroism displayed during the war and to rid the country of its degenerate ways. His purpose was to imbue Germans with the will to avenge the bitter suffering inflicted by the Jewish-inspired Versailles Peace Treaty. He urged the restoration of Germany's military power, and also called for the acquisition of living space in the East (*Lebensraum*) from states such as Poland and Russia as essential for the country's survival. In his mind such tasks were closely intertwined with the goal of attaining "The Final Solution of the Jewish Question" (Die Endlösung der Judenfrage).

Before 1933, many Germans, especially intellectuals, ridiculed *Mein Kampf* and dismissed Hitler's diatribes as the fevered rantings of a would-be-leader who couldn't even write proper German. Failure to take him seriously was a factor in his success in 1933. During the Nazi era, *Mein Kampf* became required reading for everyone. Two million copies were printed in 1935 alone.

CHAPTER 2

Family Life to 1933

The Bernsteins

We do not know how deeply the Bernstein family was affected by anti-Jewish sentiment. Its members thrived as assimilated, patriotic, and observant Jews. Paul's father, Isidor, was born in Berlin in 1852 and died in 1915. His mother, Johanna, nee Herzberg, was born in Myslowice in 1861, now in Poland, and died in 1934 in Berlin. Her sister, Regina Herzberg, who lived with the Bernsteins, was born in 1863 and died in 1942 in the Nazi Ghetto of Theresienstadt. Isidor and Johanna are buried in the large Jewish cemetery in Berlin-Weissensee, which the Nazis left alone, perhaps hoping to safeguard their international reputation. The cemetery also survived Berlin's vast number of air raids, as well as the fierce fighting in late April 1945 when the Soviets conquered the city.

The Bernsteins had long lived in Berlin. Originally, the family came from Trier in western Germany, close to the borders of Luxemburg and France. According to our mother, Paul Bernstein could trace his ancestry back to the fourteenth century. During the expulsion of Jews from west German cities, many migrated to Berlin and to Poland.

We learned only in 2013 that Isidor had a brother, Adolf Bernstein, who emigrated to the US sometime in the 1890s, and died in about 1910. He had three children, Beatrice, Regina, and Charles, who was born in 1895 and died in 1987. In 2013, we met with Charles' granddaughter, Emily Berleth, who gave us copies of three poignant letters written by Richard, Paul's elder brother, in 1939 and 1940. In these letters Richard asks his uncle for an affidavit of support required for emigration to the United States, which he supplied. The US consulate failed to issue a visa and he was murdered in Auschwitz (see Chapter 4). Barbara met other relatives of the family who live in the US, but we have not been in touch with them.

Isidor owned a brush factory and the Bernsteins were a prosperous upper-middle-class Jewish family, living in a large apartment not far from the center of the city. They owned a cottage at a lake in east Berlin, which our father, Paul, remembered fondly. Isidor was a generous and kind man who disliked injustice, even if it didn't affect him personally.

Isidor's eldest son, Richard, was born on August 9,1888, followed by Paul on June 23, 1897. Richard was educated in England, where he was interned as an enemy alien during WWI, returning home after Germany's defeat in 1918. He became a real estate broker and a manager in a major electricity company. Like his father, he was a man of rectitude who placed great value on business ethics. He was an elegant, well-groomed, and fastidious individual—very bourgeois, a real gentleman.

His younger brother, Paul, rejected bourgeois values, but was somewhat afraid of his much more conservative older brother. When the two met, he was always careful to brush his suit, select the right tie, and shine his shoes. Richard would notice the remaining flaws. Paul was tolerant of his older brother's social conservatism. Johanna Moosdorf, his wife, recalled that during visits, Paul "listened to Richard's nonsense without objecting but rolled his eyes towards her lest she explode." Richard married a non-Jewish woman, Gertrude Schroen, a formidable blond who was eleven years older. Johanna didn't like to visit Richard's parents, repelled by their apartment crammed with gaudy furniture, antiques, and Persian rugs (letter, 1966).

Johanna Bernstein, the mother of Richard and Paul, was beautiful, delicate, intelligent, well educated, socially ambitious, and rather disdainful of those she considered beneath her. Johanna's sister, Regina Herzberg, was not as good-looking nor as bright, but was tender, full of love, and in need of love. She nurtured Paul in a way that his mother did not. Paul's birth required forceps for which his mother "never forgave him" (ibid).

After Isidor's death in 1915, Paul's mother sold the brush factory and invested her "considerable wealth" in German war bonds, which lost their value after Germany's defeat. In the 1920s, in order to earn a living, Johanna and Regina converted their large apartment into a *Pension*, a small hotel for long-term guests. When Johanna got to know them, Paul's mother told her that she deeply regretted believing that Germany would win the war.

Paul had his Bar Mitzva in 1911 and was educated at an elite school, the Kaiser Friedrich Gymnasium. His mother studied Greek in order to help her son with his school work. She was very concerned about his grades, wanting him always to excel. When report cards arrived, she would phone relatives—the Rings, the Herzbergs, and the Witkowskis—to discuss their children's performance, much to Paul's chagrin. He excelled in history, Latin, and Greek, but not in French, math, and chemistry.

At one point Paul was severely scolded—not because he was Jewish, since the school did not discriminate against Jews—but because he put a cap on a bust of German Emperor Wilhelm I in the school auditorium. The principal gave him a harsh reprimand in front of the entire school: "You wicked boy, how dare you inflict this shame on the Hero Emperor!" (ibid). Why "Hero'"? As noted above, during the Franco-German war of 1871 Germany was unified, and Prussia's King Wilhelm I became emperor of the German empire. His eldest son, Wilhelm II, reigned from 1888 to 1918, the year of Germany's defeat, after which he abdicated and fled to Holland.

When WWI began, many Jews rushed to join the military. At least ten thousand volunteered. Among 1,100 Jewish university students, 991 did so (Fürst, 45). In *Comrades Betrayed: Jewish WW1 Veterans under Hitler*, Michael Geheran depicts the motives of the volunteers as wanting to demonstrate their patriotism, masculinity, and courage by risking their lives as frontline soldiers:

> To acculturated German Jews, the war represented the long-awaited moment for them to publicly demonstrate their loyalty to the fatherland and surmount the last hurdles toward complete integration in German society" (15).

In 1916, antisemitic officers propagated the canard that Jews were shirking frontline military service, prompting Emperor Wilhelm II to order a census which showed that the percentage of Jews who served at the front was at least as high as that of the non-Jewish population. But this information was kept secret. About ninety-six thousand Jews served in the military, of whom at least twelve thousand were killed in action and many more were wounded. Thirty-five thousand received medals; one Jewish soldier was awarded the highest imperial decoration for valor, the "Pour le Merite"; more than two thousand became officers, and nineteen thousand served as NCOs (Fürst, 44). During the war, no anti-Jewish riots or pogroms took place (Ozment, 277)

Other Jews held high positions in the government during the war. One of them, Walter Rathenau, directed the distribution of raw materials for the industrial war effort. A postwar minister of foreign affairs, he was assassinated by right-wing fanatics in 1922.

After Paul's graduation from high school in March 1916, he apparently was one of the many who volunteered. His mother and probably others in the family spoke of the duty he owed to his fatherland (*Pflichtgefühl*). He fought in the East and in France, where he served in the trenches. He was hospitalized three times, twice for wounds and once for dysentery, and was awarded an Iron Cross and the *Verwundetenabzeichen* (wound badge). He maintained close friendships with gentile veterans who continued to meet with him long after the 1933 Nazi takeover.

After Germany's defeat in 1918, Paul enlisted in a Freikorps unit, one of the right-wing militias that fought against Bolshevism in the Baltics and Poland and the loss of territory imposed under the Treaty of Versailles. These forces also took part in crushing the short-lived communist seizures of power in several cities and towns. Paul found that the Freikorps also aimed to restore to power of the militarist Prussian nobility (Wikipedia, "Weimar Paramilitary Groups," "Die Freikorps"). Paul quickly ended his affiliation with the Freikorps. His wife observed during his service in the east, "his love for Germany and Germans led him to dislike Ostjuden (Eastern Jews) as foreign and non-Western." Only much later, when he got to know some in Berlin, he became aware of the injustice of his views (letter, 1966).

The Moosdorfs

Our mother, Johanna Moosdorf, was born on July 12, 1911 in Leipzig and died in Berlin in 2000. Her mother, Anna Moosdorf, nee Eis, was born in 1866 and died in 1914. She was a strong-willed, independent woman who inherited a farm and was excommunicated by the Catholic Church for marrying a Protestant, Hermann Moosdorf.

Johanna's father was a self-educated printer who worked his way up to a senior position in a publishing house. He was able to typeset Egyptian hieroglyphics as well as Greek and Hebrew. Hermann collected rare books and owned a large library that our mother inherited, but which was destroyed in an air raid in 1943. His grandfather participated in the abortive Revolution of 1848. He was a member of the Social Democratic Party (SPD), but broke with it over the party's support for war credits when Germany went to war in 1914. He briefly supported the Spartacists—a far-left group that turned into the German Communist Party—but in due course returned to the SPD.

Anna's death in 1914 was a terrible blow for three-year old Johanna. After his wife's death, Hermann hired a twenty-two-year-old woman, Alice Schoenfeld, as a caregiver and maid. He married her in 1917, perhaps to stop neighbors from gossiping about them. Hermann told his daughter: "you have a new mother." Johanna went on strike, refusing to shake her stepmother's hand or to accept her. Prolonged tension between the two ensued since Alice disapproved of everything Johanna did. Her father apparently ignored the conflict, or perhaps wasn't aware of it because his daughter felt unable to tell him about her troubles with her stepmother. During WWII, she was our *Oma* (grandmother).

Hermann took good care of Johanna during WWI, when Germany suffered from acute food shortages caused by the Allied blockade. In 1917, during the "turnip winter," Johanna became anemic. Herman took her to various villages to buy food, so she was not as thin as other children. Johanna attended a secondary girl's high school whose teachers had doctorates and were called professors; some of them kindled her interest in literature. She also joined the Leipzig University Church Choir, where she sang for several years. In the 1920s she participated in the German youth movement and took part in camping trips, hikes, and group singing—activities that she later came to share with Paul Bernstein.

In 1928, Johanna's stepmother, sought to arrange a marriage for her to a "respectable" owner of a cigar store. Johanna firmly rejected the proposal. In that year she made a serious suicide attempt, having been enticed by a man who wanted to show her his art collection. He got her to come to his apartment and tried to seduce her. She repelled him, ran home, turned on the gas, and would have died had Hermann and Alice not returned home in time. She humiliated Johanna by talking about the incident with her teachers. Johanna's suicide attempt also greatly hurt her father, as did her subsequent running away from home. She went to the Habertshof Boarding School where one of her brothers, Willi, was the accountant.

Johanna's older brother, Hermann, was born in 1897 and served in WWI. She remembers him coming home on leave from the Western Front in 1917 and how deeply moved her father was. He was killed in action in July 1918. For many years he was listed as missing, and every day her father visited city hall to see whether news about his son had been posted. His remains were finally found in 1935, together with an Iron Cross.

A second brother, Uncle Willi, was born in 1903 and died in 1959. He had a legal wife, Lia Moosdorf, while another woman, Maria Correvon, lived with them and became pregnant with Willie's oldest son, Ulrich, born in 1939, whom I met in 1958. We have long had contact with Ulrich's son, Karl, born in 1965. In 2015, my daughter, Anya, her family, and I met him in Berlin. For my grandchildren, Ben and Sarah, this trip was an opportunity to learn about our family. Together, we visited the gravesites of Paul and Johanna.

The Weimar Republic, 1919–1933

Germany's sudden military collapse in 1918, largely unanticipated by the public, had a shattering impact on society. The enormous bloody and material sacrifices of the war had not yielded the hoped for benefits. The defeat greatly intensified the political cleavages of the prewar era and precipitated years of political instability, turmoil, and violence. Initially, hopes were aroused for a democratic political future. In early January, 1919 the German National Constitutional Assembly in Weimar drafted a new constitution and organized the country's first fully free elections. Remarkably, three-fourths of voters chose three moderate parties to govern, the Social Democratic Party (SPD), the Democratic Party, and the Catholic Center Party rather than voting for far-left or far-right parties. The SPD's leader, Friedrich Ebert, was chosen as the republic's first president.

But these hopes were soon dashed. A year later, the centrist coalition collapsed. The far left and far right rejected Germany's new democracy, as did mainstream conservatives, who believed that the republic should be replaced by an authoritarian regime. Their anger and hate were aimed at the new regime which had been forced to accept the Treaty of Versailles. They condemned the republic's leaders for accepting that Germany was solely responsible for the war and agreeing to pay huge reparations to the Allies. Germany's military was defanged. It was permitted an army of only one hundred thousand men and was forbidden to conscript soldiers, build submarines, and have an air force. It was also made to limit the tonnage of navy ships to no more than ten thousand. Germans widely believed that the war's victors' intended to humiliate the country and keep it in a state of permanent subjugation and impoverishment. The men who had agreed to the armistice in 1918 were denounced as "the November criminals." Some of the signees were Jewish, and so, the right scapegoated Jews for all of Germany's troubles. Antisemitism became "a staple of right-wing thought and propaganda" (Stern, 59). The Jewish foreign minister Walter Rathenau's "life exemplified the partial, embattled success of German Jewry; his murder [in 1922] exposed the country's raging passions" (65).

Renewed slanders accused Jews of having evaded military service and claimed that they had avoided fighting in the trenches. To counteract these lies, veterans in 1919 founded the Reichsbund Jüdischer Frontsoldaten (Association of Jewish Frontline Soldiers). This organization proclaimed the loyalty and sacrifice of Jewish veterans. Gentile army officers, including generals, regularly took part in commemorative gatherings, thereby publicly recognizing that Jewish soldiers had demonstrated their commitment to Germany. During the Weimar Republic, 1919–1933, between thirty to forty thousand veterans joined the organization, that is, more than half of the Jews who had served in WWI. The Reichsbund set up five hundred local branches; the largest one, in Berlin, had about five thousand members. The organization published a journal titled *Der Schild* (The Shield), which in 1932 produced a memorial book listing Jews killed in the war. Even after the Nazi seizure of power, the Reichsbund published "Wartime Letters of Fallen German Jews" (Berger, 63–64). We were not able to find out whether Paul was a member.

Weimar's endless domestic and international crises culminated in 1923: hyperinflation ruined millions; France occupied the Ruhr industrial region to enforce the payment of reparations; Adolf Hitler staged a brief violent uprising in Munich, ten years before his "legal" ascent to power, while the KPD engaged in revolutionary violence. These crises ended after a new coalition that included SPD ministers came to power and brought about a few years of relative political stability and prosperity, largely financed with American loans. Internationally, pressure on Germany declined after a rapprochement with France and its admission to the League of Nations. Alas, this golden period in Weimar's history ended in 1929 with the onset of the Great Depression. Germany was plunged into a massive economic crisis, which resulted in large-scale unemployment and widespread misery. An increasingly ineffective government failed to find effective solutions, thereby paving the way for the Nazi seizure of power in 1933 (Ozment, chapter 10; Stern, chapter 2).

The SPD had already emerged as a major political force in prewar imperial and partially democratic Germany. During the Weimar years, it became the country's largest party, took part in coalition governments, and in 1928 was able to elect a chancellor. The strength of the social democratic movement prompted a cousin of Isidor's, Eduard Bernstein, a prominent member of the SPD, to write his famous book *Evolutionary Socialism.* In it, he argued that social democratic parties in Western Europe could come to power peacefully via elections and not via violent revolutions. Communists vehemently rejected this claim, beginning with Vladimir Lenin, the Bolshevik leader, who led his party to power in the October Revolution of 1917. Eduard died in 1932.

Paul Bernstein, 1919–1931

After the war, Paul's mother, Johanna Bernstein, used her contacts with the directors of a large, Jewish-owned enterprise to get Paul a job as an executive-in-training. Paul made good money but didn't stay, causing his mother to despair. He probably left because of his anti-capitalist convictions and also perhaps because he was embarrassed by the favoritism shown him. Instead, he enrolled at the Deutsche Hochschule für Politik (College for Political Studies), a private institution which in 1959 was incorporated into the Free University of Berlin. He studied there until 1930 and did so well that the received a fellowship to study the League of Nations in Geneva and where he met Alice Hanson Cook who was studying at a German university.

A strong letter of recommendation states that he was qualified for further study (that is, for a doctorate) and to teach in Germany's highly developed system of adult education. He became a passionate, dedicated, and exciting teacher of young workers who enrolled in short courses at trade union venues and the Habertshof Heimvolkshochschule (Higher People's Boarding School). Paul lectured on topics such as the history of Germany's Peasant War of 1525, the French Revolution, the working-class movement, the philosophy of Hegel, and Marxist theory. The school's educational goals were based on the ideas of Protestant religious socialism. This approach sought to nurture progressive attitudes, study the struggles of the working class, and commit to finding solutions to the severe crises then afflicting Germany. Teaching methods were not politically neutral; instead, students were encouraged to take sides on particular issues. Political differences, it was believed, could be moderated by respectful, thoughtful, and factually based arguments. This required close cooperation between teachers and students and a narrowing of the barrier between them. While studying, students lived and worked together in order to foster solidarity (Blum). Paul found this educational philosophy very attractive. The Nazis closed it down in 1933.

Karl Moosdorf, whose grandmother and grandfather had been administrators at the school told me about Habertshof. During the Nazi years, Johanna's brother, Willi, and others who had worked there came under suspicion. Willi's family was strongly opposed to the Nazis, and some of its members smuggled Jewish valuables and documents to Holland. During the war, Willi was arrested because "he talked too much and told the wrong jokes in front of wrong people." He was tried by the Volksgerichtshof (People's Court), but "some testimonies" saved him." Karl thinks his release may have been due to his enlisting in the military. He went on to serve as a medic in Russia (Karl Moosdorf, e-mail, June 18, 2023).

As an SPD activist, Paul wrote for a monthly journal for young socialist workers, *Sozialistische Arbeiter Jugend.* I acquired sixteen articles (located by Amelie Döge) that were published between 1929 and 1932. These are short, but trenchant, essays that deal with topics including the British and French labor movements, the political crisis in Austria, the danger of a new war, and the necessity of reaching an understanding with France.

In the journal's June 1930 issue, Paul examined the origins and development of the Nazi Party, its racist ideology, program, and organization. He wrote that a major source of popular support came from people in the lower middle class who were deprived of a secure future when their small businesses went bankrupt during the Great Depression. Paul noted that their despair and hopelessness was widely shared by the unemployed. Young people, whose belief in a real future was shattered by the economic crisis, succumbed to Nazi propagandists, who blamed Jews for their plight.

In the parliamentary elections in September 1930, the Nazis increased the number of their deputies in the Reichstag (parliament) from twelve to 107, and thus moved from the fringes to the center of politics (Wikipedia, "1930 German Federal Election data"). The SPD's contingent of 143 deputies was still larger, however. Paul observed that Nazi propaganda inveighed against capitalism, taking advantage of growing popular disenchantment with the current economic system. The name of the party, the National Socialist German Workers Party, signified its intent to pursue some kind of a pro-labor program. Its propagandists made skillful efforts to mobilize disillusioned working-class and lower-middle-class voters, but Paul believed that the Nazi Party was actually under the thumb of big business, and argued that the party's promises were fraudulent. Stern, however, proposes that few Marxists "understood that the real power of the National Socialists lay in their brilliantly organized pseudo-religious emotional appeal" (Stern, 78).

Paul understood that the Nazis' fanatical nationalism appealed to voters whose suffering could not be alleviated due to the enormous sums owed to the Allies. He wrote that Moscow had ordered the KPD to join the Nazis in putting forth sweeping nationalist demands for the abrogation of the Treaty of Versailles. He contended that the KPD had gained seats in the Reichstag because many people didn't comprehend the policies of the SPD, now the only defender of democracy. The SPD, he concluded, should prepare for struggle outside of parliament.

In 1930, Paul encouraged Alice Hanson Cook to spend a semester at the Berlin College for Politics. She had gone to Germany to do graduate work on subjects that were Paul's specialty—adult education and trade unions—and also to learn about the internationally renowned SPD. Alice quickly became aware of the remarkable success of the Nazis in the September elections. From the visitors' gallery of the Reichstag, she watched as Nazi deputies wearing their brownshirt uniforms marched into the chamber giving the Hitler salute. As she wrote in her autobiography: "In this atmosphere my political consciousness rose to a fever pitch, that resulted in my inscribing myself as a student member of the SPD, a commitment to socialism that I carried over to the United States (Cook, 67). She witnessed SA storm troopers throwing stones at the windows of Jewish department stores and disrupting KPD and SPD meetings. On one occasion, when she and Paul were dining in a restaurant, a man walked by their table and dropped a handwritten note warning her "against any public appearance with a dirty Jew." At a rally led by the Nazis' propaganda chief Josef Goebbels, Alice and a friend "both booed and were threatened by a guard with expulsion" (68). Nevertheless, she persisted in believing that the trade unions and the SDP would be able to "prevent the ultimate disaster that came only two years later" (69). She left Germany in 1931 because she lacked funding, and took a job in Philadelphia with the YWCA.

Johanna and Paul in Berlin, 1931–1933

Johanna met Paul at Harbertshof and attended a lecture of his that enthralled her. They soon fell in love. Now twenty, she was attractive, lively, poetic, and romantic. Paul was fourteen years older, a political activist, and a teacher. The two shared intellectual interests and believed in the importance of having a Weltanschauung.

They were also different. In *Dreams of the Century,* Johanna describes herself as an idealist and somewhat distant from reality. Paul had a more realistic outlook and was deeply involved in political activities and current events. The two shared literary interests, but while she loved the deep moodiness of Russian novels, he was more oriented to the Western world, thinking of the Bolshevik Revolution as something very alien and eastern. Johanna got him to appreciate Dostoyevsky, Yiddish stories, and poetry. "We gave each other a lot," Johanna writes.

When Johanna arrived in Berlin in the late summer of 1931, she and Paul witnessed a clash between SA and counterdemonstrators, and, as he had done earlier with Alice Cook, Paul shoved her into a doorway to protect her from the violence. The SA surrounded the crowd and two of their bullies stopped him from leaving, forcing Paul's arm up in the Hitler salute. (*Dreams,* 103).

By then, Johanna had become an ardent feminist, telling Paul that she couldn't love someone who demanded subordination and obedience from women. Paul's outlook was more traditional; he was chivalrous and protective of women, but promised that he would fully respect her views.

In 1932, Johanna had a miscarriage and had to be hospitalized. The doctors and nurses were conservative, antisemitic nationalists, but apparently not Nazis. They wanted her to charge Paul with rape, but in the end the staff came to accept him. He successfully insisted that Johanna be given an anesthetic, which was not normally done for poor women.

Johanna saw in Paul a strong, good-natured individual who was always cheerful (*heiter*), easily able to charm people, steadfast, uncomplaining, and accustomed to hardship He was never ill-tempered or grumpy. He was good humored and had a strong sense of irony. When he told complicated jokes and anecdotes, he would laugh uproariously. He liked light music and opera, and at one point was hired as an opera extra. During a performance of *Aida,* dressed as an Egyptian gatekeeper, he got carried away by the music and swung his arms like the conductor. While watching a silent comedy he laughed with such enthusiasm that the audience joined him, prompting the movie house manager to offer him free tickets.

Paul wanted badly to be accepted as a regular German. "He never mentioned that he felt undervalued as a Jew but felt more German than Jewish" (1966 letter). Before 1933, he was not close to the Jewish community, but he did not convert to Christianity, despite the fact that for many years, a good many Jews had done so. His dual identity as a German and a Jew was not affected even after the Nazis took away his German citizenship and made Jews "state subjects." He was aware of the missteps in German history, but remained tolerant and fundamentally uncritical of the country. In a 1931 letter to Alice Hanson Cook, who had just returned to the US, he mentions that the Depression had damaged his livelihood:

> but I hope that the Lord who nurtures the lilies and makes the grass grow won't let me starve, which would do irreparable damage to the workers' movement. And then I am, after all, a German even though Herr Hitler would doubt this. You won't argue with me that the Germans are looking toward their ruin with great patience. No other people in the world would turn on the gas in so calm a state.

Paul had a remarkable talent for communicating with poorly educated people, and was able to convey complex ideas without condescending to them. He spent "countless hours" with his frontline comrades, patiently listening to their family problems even though he was not really interested in them. Johanna recalls that when he spoke at meetings in Berlin with Nazis in the audience he countered their catcalls with "true brilliance and, despite his Jewishness, no violence ensued. . . . I don't know whether it was luck or whether it reflected his talent for getting across to the dumbest" (1966 letter).

In 1932, the Berlin City Council Senate and German trade unions jointly funded a home for young unemployed workers and authorized Paul and Johanna to run it, provided they formally married—a demand with which they complied, despite their disdain for bourgeois customs. Paul's mother, Johanna, initially disapproved of Paul's marriage to a young Christian woman, but she came to love her daughter-in-law and told Paul to protect her. Others in the Bernstein family shared these feelings. After Barbara and I were born, Aunt Regina asked whether we were being raised properly as Jews. Our mother remembered both sisters as lively and interesting old ladies.

The workers' home hosted sixteen men and three women. A trade union provided two floors of a union-owned house, as well as beds, blankets, and equipment for a workshop containing tools for carpentry and metal work. The workers made objects for everyday use. After their marriage, Johanna and Paul dissolved the old Bernstein apartment and donated its furniture to the home (Entschädigungsamt—Restitution Office). Our parents engaged the group in a variety of activities, including discussions of the current political crisis.

Despite the increasingly ominous political situation, the couple was happy and very busy during 1932. Paul wrote six articles for the *Sozialistische Arbeiter Jugend* and was appointed to teach as a *Dozent* (lecturer) at the Berlin Higher School for Adult Education. He continued to speak at SPD meetings and was active in the organization. Johanna led youth groups and lectured on literature. She wrote poems which a newly established publishing house agreed to publish, but in 1933 this offer was rescinded because of her marriage to a Jew. The couple was poor, but managed with earnings from honoraria and lecture fees.

Paul's last published article in 1932, "Reaction Dominates Germany," contrasted the historic English Reform Act of 1832, when the ruling aristocracy agreed to expand the franchise to the middle classes, with the reactionary plans of conservatives then in power that sought to reduce the political influence of the poorer classes in Germany. These conservative proposals came to nothing, when the Nazis seized power in January 1933 and imposed their one-party dictatorship that mobilized the masses from above.

The KPD bitterly opposed the rise of the Nazis, believing that the hoped-for revolution would break out soon after the Nazi collapse it anticipated. Their slogan, "it will be our turn after Hitler" (Nach Hitler kommen wir) turned out to be a tragic delusion. In 1928, the Soviet dictator, Joseph Stalin, ordered the world's communist parties not to form "united fronts" with other parties, labelling democratic socialist parties "social fascists." As Stern writes:

> Inevitably the Communists proved profiteers of the capitalist collapse, which seemingly confirmed a Leninist prognosis. And the fears aroused by communist successes made

> conservative *Bürger* (bourgeoisie) look to the National Socialists for protection [a case] of opposing extremists' aid each other (84).

As a result, the communists actually helped Hitler gain power. Stalin changed his tune in 1935 in favor of multiparty united fronts because the threat of fascism loomed ever larger in the world.

On January 30, 1933, President Hindenburg appointed Adolf Hitler Chancellor of a coalition government of conservatives and Nazis. He acted in accord with Article 48 of the Weimar Constitution, which permitted the president to use his powers of decree in cases of dire national emergency. He did so because intense political conflicts made it impossible to form a parliamentary coalition able to pass the laws that were urgently needed if Germany was to recover from the Depression. As Levitsky and Ziblatt have pointed out in their book *Why Democracies Die* (2018), a critical cause of Hitler's triumph was the failure of conservatives to defend democracy from far-right radicals. The German conservatives who promoted Hitler's appointment did so because they thought that Hitler had the necessary mass support to break the political gridlock: "They despised him but at least they knew he had a mass following. And most of all, they thought they could control him. . . . We've engaged him for ourselves. Within two months, we will have pushed him so far into a corner that he'll squeal" (14–15). Another conservative later remarked that "I have just committed the greatest stupidity of my life; I have allied myself with the greatest demagogue in world history" (19). And indeed, the Nazis soon prevailed over them as he consolidated his dictatorship. "Hitler, the man of violence, rhetorically dissolved political complexity into a Wagnerian battle between the pure and the impure, between German heroes and Jewish-Marxist traitors" (Stern, 85).

Six days before the last more or less free elections were held on March 5, 1933, the Nazis set the Reichstag on fire, but lied that it was a treasonous KPD attempt to overthrow the government. Hitler persuaded President Hindenburg to issue an emergency decree against the communists. The party was outlawed and thousands of its leaders arrested. All over Germany, Storm troopers, the SS and police auxiliaries were ordered to supervise the elections, creating an atmosphere of intimidation and fear. Members of anti-Nazi parties were harassed, beaten, had their publications suppressed, or were arrested. In Prussia, long an SPD stronghold, Hermann Göring, then the acting minister of the interior, issued an order authorizing the police to use force against political opponents (Wikipedia, "March 1933 German federal election").

Despite the terror, the Nazi Party failed to win a majority on March 5, 1933. It received just 43.9% of the votes and added ninety-two deputies to their Reichstag contingent for a total 288 seats, its best showing ever. The SPD came in second, getting 18.3% and 120 deputies. The KPD, already outlawed, received 12.3%, but their eighty-one deputies had either gone underground or were in prison. The middle-of-the road Center Party won only 11.25%, adding three Reichstag deputies, for a total of seventy-tree. The three main opposition parties thus had 274 deputies, including the now absent communists. Hitler continued as chancellor but with only a bare majority.

Hitler now demanded adoption of the Enabling Act "A Decree for the Removal of Distress from German People and Reich," but its passage required a two-thirds Reichstag majority. This time, the Center Party supported the Nazis and the decree was passed on March 23, 1933, with 444 votes. Only the ninety-four remaining SPD deputies opposed it. This law ended democracy in Germany (ibid).

Members of the young workers' collective that our parents were administering watched as the Reichstag was set on fire. They listened to Paul's final talk about the deadly danger posed by the end of democracy, "the only political system that could uphold human dignity" (*Dreams*, 96). The workers debated how to respond to the Nazis' onslaught; some sided with them, but most wanted to resist. They waited for a call by the SPD leadership to mobilize the party's own militia, the Reichsbanner, organized during the Weimar years to fight far-right violence. But the SPD's leaders failed to issue such a command and did not offer sustained organized resistance against Hitler's seizure of power.

On May 1, SA members forcibly hoisted a swastika on the roof of the workers' collective. Johanna went to a nearby police precinct to complain to its captain, who was not a Nazi. He agreed that this was a case of breach of the peace (*Hausfriedensbruch*) and ordered the banner's removal. After he threatened to impose a fine on the SA group, they complied. Later, an SA mob stormed the collective's building, doing much damage. Two weeks later, the home was closed, this time without police intervention. and in May the collective shuttered for good.

During the Nazi takeover, the SA set up many makeshift jails for its political enemies, torturing them at will. These facilities were soon replaced by state-run concentration camps. Paul and Johanna learned that friends had been incarcerated in one of them. They phoned the place pretending to be SA; they claimed that a mistake had been made and that they should be released, which they were. As late as May 1933, Paul collected an honorarium for an article in a trade union paper *Holzarbeiter Zeitung* (Woodworkers' Paper), in the presence of suspicious Storm troopers. At that time, the Nazis dissolved all trade unions and replaced them with the German Workers' Front (1966 letter).

CHAPTER 3

From Persecution to Genocide, 1933–1945

Persecution, 1933–1941

The census of 1933 reported that 522,000 religious Jews lived in Germany, not including Christian converts, those who had left the Jewish community, or who were living in mixed marriages ("Documenting . . . the victims"). This complicated the Nazis' self-imposed task of determining who was Jewish.

In April 1933, the regime called for a boycott of Jewish-owned department stores. The slogan, "Deutsche, wehrt euch, kauft nicht von Juden" (Germans, defend yourselves, don't buy from Jews) expressed the Nazis' siege mentality. The aim was to separate Jews from German institutions and society, turn them into pariahs, and force them to emigrate. A great many Germans, though by no means all, came to believe in the Nazi propaganda that sought to inculcate hatred, contempt, and disgust towards Jews encouraged by these slogans: "Die Juden sind unser Unglück" (The Jews are our misfortune) and "Die Juden sind an allem schuld" (The Jews are guilty of everything). The Hitler Youth sang, "Wenn Judenblut vom Messer spritzt, dann gehts nochmal so gut" (When Jewish blood splatters from the knife, things go even better).

Jews were dismissed from the civil service, universities, and from other key institutions. Many were forced to sell their businesses to Aryans at fire-sale prices, which led to their growing impoverishment. The 1935 race laws prohibited marriage between Aryans and Jews, who were labelled "state subjects," that is, noncitizens (Noakes). In 1938, Jews were ordered to acquire new identity cards bearing the letter "J," and were forced to add "the typically Jewish-sounding" names of Sara and Israel to their own.

Jews were subjected to a cascade of prohibitions, restrictions, and exclusions that were humiliating and often petty. They were not allowed to sit on park benches reserved for Aryans, although such signs were temporarily removed during the 1936 Berlin Olympic Games lest they offend foreigners. Jews could no longer use Aryan sports facilities or eat in railroad dining cars. Numerous towns posted signs stating that "Jews are not wanted here."

Enforcement of these measures required the cooperation of government agencies, educational institutions, businesses, and the public at large. The Nazis encouraged denunciations and antisemitic local initiatives before official rules had been promulgated. Many officials and ordinary people acted "im Sinne des Führers" (working towards the Führer) in accordance with what they thought Hitler would want to be done. This added unpredictability and uncertainty to the process of repression (Kershaw, *Hubris*, 530–531).

The severity of the repression escalated sharply when, on November 9 and 10, 1938, the Nazis staged a nationwide orgy of violence, *Kristallnacht* (the Night of Broken Glass). An eruption of rage, it was meant to avenge the assassination of a German diplomat in Paris by a Jew who was angered by his father's persecution. Mobs of Nazis and ordinary citizens burned down synagogues, looted and destroyed Jewish-owned department stores, and beat and arrested Jews. Thirty thousand Jews were sent to concentration camps, where they were exposed to extraordinary cruelty. The police were instructed not to interfere. *Kristallnacht* unleashed "two days of terror that those who survived would never forget" (Geheran, 119). A fine of a billion Reichsmarks was imposed on the Jewish community as collective punishment, causing ever deeper impoverishment.

When WWII started in September, 1939, Jews were regarded as threat to national security, and their persecution intensified. They were evicted from their residences and forced to move into *Judenhäuser* (Jew houses). They had to turn in radios, were forbidden to speak to soldiers, and were subjected to a curfew from 8:00 pm to 5:00 am. Gestapo (Geheime Staatspolizei; Secret State Police) officials searched for weapons and other signs of "enemy activity," ordeals that are vividly described in the diaries of Victor Klemperer, a fired Jewish professor, *Ich will Zeugnis ablegen bis zum letzten* (I want to bear Witness to the last). A directive threatened Germans who continued to have Jewish friends with temporary imprisonment for "education" and, in "serious cases," with up to three months in a concentration camp (Geheran, 133). In 1940, Jews were ordered to perform forced labor and a year later to wear the *Judenstern* (Jewish star), further subjecting them to public abuse. In 1942, they were forbidden to buy white bread, milk, meat, or fruit, and forced to give up their pets, telephones, binoculars, and much else.

Draconian punishments were imposed on those who resisted. In 1942, a Jewish underground group of communist youths led by Herbert Baum set fire to a public exhibit in Berlin that depicted the horrors of Stalin's "Soviet paradise." Adolf Eichman, the head of the SS Department of Jewish Affairs, informed the Reichsvereinigung der Juden in Deutschland (the National Association of Jews in Germany) about the "revenge action" that followed: Baum took his own life, but his accomplices were executed. Five hundred Berlin Jews were arrested, of whom half were shot and the rest sent to concentration camps (Wikipedia, "Herbert Baum"; Longerich, 1989, "Meldung", 405–406).

Emigration

Persecution sought to compel Jews to leave Germany, thereby "cleansing German living space by legal means" (*Wannsee*). But the conditions of their departure were extremely onerous. In order to secure exit permits, Jews had to pay a "flight tax" (*Reichsfluchtsteuer*), sell their property, and overcome numerous obstacles imposed by Nazi bureaucrats; only occasionally did bribery work. Moreover, many of the countries to which Jews hoped to escape set restrictive quotas or forbade entry altogether (Kaplan). After *Kristallnacht,* many more Jews made frantic efforts to leave. Despite all obstacles, by the time emigration was officially forbidden in October 1941, about 360,000 Jews, more than half the German Jewish population in 1933, succeeded in emigrating, 140,000 of them to the United States. Many of those who escaped to countries in Western Europe were later murdered during the Holocaust.

Temporary Exemptions for Jewish WWI Veterans

The ascriptive label of Jews as a "race" and not simply a religion meant that personal "merit" was not, in principle, a factor in determining anyone's fate. But in the case of WWI veterans, many Germans believed that Jews who had fought in the war, especially those who had been decorated, wounded, or disabled, deserved special consideration, since they had demonstrated their loyalty to their fatherland. "The 'Wound Badge' was a symbol of immense social prestige in Nazi Germany" (Geheran, 177). Segments of the military agreed that the persecution of veterans violated the corporate honor of the army and negated the comradeship that Jews and gentiles shared when fighting together in the trenches.

Despite such support, in the violence that accompanied the Nazi takeover, Jewish veterans were targeted during the April 1, 1933, boycott of Jewish department stores. In response, some veterans wore their medals to shame the young Storm Troopers standing guard in front of these stores. In the same month, a draft civil service law called for the dismissal of Jews, prompting the aged German president Hindenburg, whose wartime accomplishments were widely celebrated, and who shared the hostility of many conservatives towards Jews, nonetheless protested to Hitler, whom he had just appointed chancellor:

> It is intolerable [that] Jewish civil servants who had been disabled in the war should suffer such treatment. . . . As far as my feelings are concerned, officials, judges, teachers, and lawyers who are war invalids, fought at the front, are the sons of war dead, or themselves lost sons in the war should remain in their positions. . . . If they were worthy of fighting and bleeding for Germany, they must also be worthy of continuing to the fatherland in their profession (Quoted in Geheran, 69).

Hitler knew that without Hindenburg's support "he could never get the army's backing, which he needed to stay in power," so he added an amendment that exempted from dismissal any individual "who participated in a battle, in trench fighting or a siege" (70). Hindenburg's death in 1934, was a blow to Jewish hopes that high-level support for veterans would continue (Berger, 67–68).

Still, as late as 1935, an Honor Cross was handed out to all frontline veterans in Hitler's name, including to Jewish veterans. In the same year, however, the Reichsbund Juedischer Frontsoldaten (Association of Jewish Frontline Soldiers) recognized that the race laws that had recently passed blocked further efforts to secure a privileged position for Jewish veterans. The Reichbund's leader submitted a petition backed by a thousand former frontline officers to the minister in charge of the armed forces, but received no response. The Bund then contacted British veteran groups, asking for help in facilitating emigration. A year later, the Gestapo restricted the Bund's role to the care of veterans wounded in battle, and, after *Kristallnacht,* it stopped functioning altogether, together with other Jewish organizations (Berger, 68–70). Nevertheless, a good many Germans stuck to the distinction between worthy veterans and ordinary Jews, including some of those who approved or tolerated the continuing persecution of nonveteran Jews and even backed the Holocaust.

During *Kristallnacht,* however, mobs didn't differentiate between ordinary Jews and veterans. "Race was the sole and explicit reason for arrests" (Geheran, 122). One party district leader, for instance, tore off a veteran's medals, "grinding them into the dirt" before sending him to Dachau concentration camp (121). SS guards in concentration camps mercilessly brutalized veterans, especially those who insisted that they had demonstrated their loyalty to Germany.

Geheran vividly depicts the steadfast attitudes and stellar behavior of many of these former soldiers during their incarceration. They bolstered the morale of despairing prisoners who had given up hope of survival (128). They drew on memories of their wartime hardships to sustain themselves as they endured the "unspeakable privations" of camp life, relying on their male self-worth and self-reliance, their ability to remain calm and composed, and their refusal to "be cowed into passive submission." They thereby preserved "the narrative of Jewish heroism" (126). Even during the Holocaust some Jewish veterans adhered to this code.

Hermann Göring, a member of Hitler's inner circle who had a distinguished war record, was chief of the Luftwaffe and held other major positions. He ordered the release of Jewish veterans from the camps even as he was issuing decrees in his capacity as the Führer's Plenipotentiary for the Final Solution to step up forced emigration and to intensify persecution of non-veteran Jews.

After their ordeal,

> Veterans . . . tried to preserve the narrative of Jewish assimilation and national belonging underpinned by military wartime sacrifice, and with it, their sense of dignity. Anything less would have meant that the comradeship and sense of oneness with other Germans had been an illusion, that Jewish sacrifices in World War I had been in vain (129).

They continued to distinguish between the German people and the Nazis and were grateful that some sheltered them or even facilitated their emigration. Others, however, noticed the "gradual numbing of the [German] soul" as people got used to the persecutions (133). After emigrating, many served in Allied armies during World War II (see also Geheran's concluding chapter 6, "Defiant Germanness").

Petitions to grant exemptions to Jewish veterans continued to be submitted by high-ranking military and civilian officials, including party members as well as members of the public. One example was Lieutenant Ernst Hess, a Jew who had served with Hitler in the same regiment and was for a time his superior officer. Hitler initially rejected Hess's petition for relief, but in 1940 ordered that a protective letter (*Schutzbrief*) be issued for him. Heinrich Himmler, the Reichsführer-SS and the head of the impending extermination program, informed the Düsseldorf chief of police "that Hess had been granted immunity from deportation" and could omit "Israel" from his name in official correspondence. But in May 1941, as deportations to the east began, the Gestapo told Hess that his special status "had been rescinded" and that he was now "a Jew like any other." Still, rather than being sent to his death, he was imprisoned in a forced labor camp and lived to see liberation (140–41).

Mixed Marriages and their *Mischling* Offspring

The Nazi obsession with the purity of German blood led to the legal prohibition of sexual relations between gentiles and Jews in the Nuremberg Race Law of 1935. Violators were charged with *Rassenschande* (race defilement). Punishments inflicted on the Jewish partner could include imprisonment and death. Interracial unions were outlawed. Aryans already married to Jews were pressured to divorce their spouses. The treatment of those who refused to comply, however, was complicated because of the feared impact of persecution on non-Jewish relatives. Mixed couples were therefore placed into a privileged category, meaning exemption from having to wear the yellow star and from other degrading regulations, such as having to live on Jewish ration cards (Kaplan, 85).

What to do about mixed-blood offspring was a complex issue to which Hitler and bureaucrats in party and state agencies devoted an extraordinary amount of time, a process depicted in excruciating detail by Noakes (291–345). The census of 1939 put the number of half-Jews at 52,005. They were classified as *Mischlinge* of the first degree because they had two Jewish grandparents. 32,669 had only one Jewish grandparent were *Mischlinge* of the second degree.

Fervent Nazis believed that *Mischlinge* should be treated as full Jews. Kaplan quotes an official as saying that the children of mixed marriages "are our greatest danger" as threats to the Aryan purity of Germans (Kaplan, 69). But some civil servants opposed this for various instrumental reasons, such as the administrative burdens that would arise when decisions had to be made about each case. Others pointed to the impact on the morale of Aryan relatives and the public and to the likely economic disruptions and difficulties in meeting military recruitment targets. Some argued that the numbers were so small that Jewish blood would soon dissolve within the German population.

With regard to second-degree *Mischlinge*, the authorities agreed that they could be integrated into the German *Volksgemeinschaft* (folkish community), provided that they satisfied a number of subjective criteria (Noakes, 316). One of these was whether an individual looked or behaved in ways thought to be typical of Jews; another was whether the shape of their skulls looked Jewish; a third was whether he or she practiced the Jewish faith. Did a *Mischling* or his or her father fight in WWI or have a record of meritorious service to the Nazi regime? Quarter-Jews were allowed to serve in the military, but could not be promoted. Decisions in each case required elaborate, intrusive investigations and might involve consultation with academic "experts" on "race".

Decisions were often arbitrary, and prompted a large number of appeals for exemptions. Some of these reached Hitler, who reserved judgment, as in the case of Ernst Hess, noted above, who was a full Jew A a distinguished Luftwaffe general, Erhard Milch continued to serve despite a Gestapo finding that his father was Jewish, prompting his boss, Hermann Göring, to remark, "*Wer Jude ist bestimme ich*" (I decide who is a Jew, Koop). Some half-Jews served in the Nazi military and some were even decorated, but all were ousted in 1941 (*Krüger*). Most petitions were apparently turned down.

During the Holocaust, the question of what to do about Jewish spouses arose once again. On January 20, 1942, SS General Heydrich, the head of the Security Service and a key planner of the genocide, convened a conference at Wannsee, a Berlin suburb, to decide on particular issues about the ongoing genocide (Longerich, 1989, "Vorbereitung", 63–73). With regard to first-degree *Mischlinge*, the conference decided that those who had been granted exemptions from evacuation to the east by the highest agencies of party and state were to be reexamined, which could well lead to abrogation of their protected status. And in order to prevent reproduction and finally to solve the *Mischling* problem, Heydrich proposed that those who "voluntarily" submitted to sterilization would not be evacuated and would be freed from the other restrictions imposed on Jews. He thought most would choose this option.

During the ensuing discussions, State Secretary of the Ministry of the Interior Dr. Stuckart suggested forcible sterilization as a simpler solution. But the procedure would require ten days of hospitalization for seventy thousand individuals, at a time when hospitals were already filled with soldiers wounded in the war against the Soviet Union. Implementation would have to await the Nazi victory (Wannsee, 65–73).

Genocide

On January 30, 1939, Hitler addressed the Reichstag and proclaimed that

> if international finance Jewry within Europe once again succeeds in plunging the peoples into a world war, the result will not be the victory of Jewry but the extermination (*Vernichtung*) of the Jewish race in Europe. (*Prolonged stormy applause.*) (Wannsee)

This prediction became a poster displayed by all Nazi Party branches (Kershaw, *Nemesis*, 442), and in 1942 the Führer repeated his "prophecy" four times. He told a large audience that although Jewry had instigated WWII in order to exterminate the Aryan peoples of Europe, the opposite would happen: "The Jews once laughed about my prophecies. I don't know whether they are still laughing. . . . Of those who laughed, untold numbers are no longer laughing. I can assure you that in time they will all stop laughing" (Ibid).

The Wannsee Conference sought to achieve clarity on "fundamental matters" pertaining to the Final Solution by coordinating SS policies with numerous state ministries, such as the Ministry of Foreign Affairs, the Ministry of the Interior, the Ministry of the Economy, and the Ministry of the Judiciary. Heydrich told his audience that about eleven million Jews were living in Europe, including those in states not then occupied by Germany. He called for

> combing through Europe from west to east to round up Jews who would then be sent to the occupied east. Those able to work would build roads, though most would likely die in the process. The hardiest survivors among them would then have to be treated "appropriately" since they might become the source of a "Jewish revival" (Ibid, 41).

Hitler ordered that no further veteran exemptions be allowed "regardless of circumstances. . . . [T]hese swine got their decorations fraudulently" (Geheran, 142, 144). In a secret conversation, Hitler admitted that "there were Jews among us who refrained from any measure directed against Germandom . . . [G]reat suffering will undoubtedly fall upon them as a result of our policy. . . . But such Jews were not conscious of the destructive character of their being" (Ibid, 174–5). Altogether, between 160,000–180,000 German Jews were murdered, of whom 55,696 had lived in Berlin (Culman, "Documenting").

Yet interventions on behalf of wounded or highly decorated veterans continued. In February 1941, the SS in Vienna rounded up a group of officer war invalids who were 50% disabled for "resettlement," leading a group of high-level military and civilian Nazis to appeal to the OKW to intervene on their behalf. The OKW apparently agreed but only in "particularly serious cases." Just twelve out of the fifty eligible Vienna officers received exemptions (Geheran, 142–43).

Later, two decorated Jewish war invalids, Fritz Arnold and Julius Fliess, told Helmut James Moltke from the military and Hans von Dohnanyi from the *Abwehr* (military counterintelligence) about their impending deportation to the Nazi ghetto at Minsk, Byelorussia. They were "disgusted" by the failure of the OKW to intervene on behalf of wounded veterans. Moltke and Dohnanyi persuaded General Herman Reinecke and Admiral Wilhelm Canaris, the head of the Abwehr, to sign a petition on behalf of wounded veterans, which the High Command accepted. Moltke told General Reinecke that he "had secured a veto by the OKW." Reinecke "personally drove to Eichmann's office to demand that these names be stricken from the list, which they were." But it is not clear whether the exemptions for Arnold and Fliess were actually extended to other wounded veterans. Geheran suggests that as late as November 1941 such interventions "were a decisive factor" in halting some deportations and that the "army was still able to persuasively articulate its moral indignation against Nazi policy in terms of honor and shame" (147).

Dohnanyi had long been committed to resist the Nazi regime. He "became close to the Wehrmacht officers who in 1938 were appalled by the prospect of war over Czechoslovakia and were determined to remove Hitler from power to avert this reckless adventure." However, at the Munich Conference held in September 1938, appeasement by the British and French governments averted war, but only for one year. During the Holocaust, the military resisters "realized that the crimes committed in Germany's name would burden that nation with inextinguishable guilt." In March 1943, Canaris and Dohnanyi attempted but failed to kill the Führer. He decreed their execution in April 1945 (Sifton and Stern). Helmut Moltke was also put to death.

In order to stop the continuing interventions by army elites and members of the public, the Wannsee Conference "decreed that war-wounded and war-decorated veterans could not be deported to the East," but would be sent to the supposedly privileged Theresienstadt Ghetto (Geheran, 170) to live out their lives in peace and quiet. This tactic allowed the Nazis to "gain exceptional leverage over ordinary Germans, including those involved in genocide" (186). In reality, conditions in Theresienstadt were terrible (see Chapter 4).

Despite this decision, Wilhem Kube, the Nazi boss of occupied Belarus, who had boasted to a superior that "55,000 local Jews had been liquidated over a ten-week period," voiced "shock" in November 1942 to find that some inmates of the Minsk Ghetto were "Jewish frontline veterans with the Iron Cross First and Second Class, war wounded, half-Aryans," implying that they should not be harmed (145).

The SS had two views regarding Jewish veterans. One was that those who staffed Jewish Order Police units in the ghettos were useful when they applied their military training to impose discipline and obedience on non-veteran inmates, thereby assisting the SS overlords to control and manage them. The second view was more ominous: Jewish veterans might be able to organize resistance to their captors, which was feared by the SS in the Minsk Ghetto. But then the SS learned that "the Order Service of the German Jews, comprising mainly former soldiers, was determined to wage armed resistance during a major clearing operation . . . in order to prevent bloodshed on the German side." The SS summarily shot them. "This was also fate of the Latvian Jewish police in Riga" after the SS found "a secret weapons cache" (140). And in the fall of 1944, veterans in Theresienstadt were for the most part deported and murdered in Auschwitz, because Himmler feared that their military training would enable them to support Czech partisans in an anticipated uprising (see Chapter 4).

The mass murder of Jews began with the occupation of Poland in 1939, when they were forced into ghettos, where tens of thousands perished from ill treatment, starvation, and disease. Browning's *Ordinary Germans* demonstrates that regular police units took part in massacres in Poland and Russia. In 1941–1942, four camps were set up in Poland designed purely for killing. Since the able-bodied were included, some military proposed keeping Jews alive to work for the German war effort, an idea that largely failed (Pasher). In September 1942, Field Marshal Wilhelm Keitel, the head of the OKW, ordered that Jewish forced laborers be replaced by ethnic Poles (Longerich, 2008, Himmler, 592).

In the wake of the invasion of the Soviet Union in June 1941, SS Einsatzgruppen (action units) operating in the huge conquered territories, went from place to place rounding up Jews and shooting them. The army provided logistical support. Erich von Manstein, the commander of the Eleventh Army, said in Russia in November 1941: "The German soldier must show sympathy for the necessity of the hard atonement (*Sühne*) demanded of Jewry, the spiritual bearer of the Bolshevik terror" (Kershaw, *Nemesis*, 466).

Auschwitz-Birkenau, an immense fifth camp in Poland, incarcerated both gentiles and Jews, from Germany and the occupied areas. This camp allowed some able-bodied persons to survive, but deaths from work and cruel treatment, called "Vernichtung durch Arbeit" (extermination by work), claimed the lives of huge numbers of inmates. In 1942, the SS innovated the use of a potent insecticide, Zyklon B, which released lethal gas in closed chambers. Tried out first on Soviet prisoners of war, it became the method of choice for killing Jews, whose bodies were incinerated in crematoriums attached to the gas chamber buildings. According to an SS report dated June 26, 1943, all five crematoria then in operation in the camp could cremate 4,756 corpses every twenty-four hours (Danuta, 429).

On October 4, 1943, Himmler spoke to a gathering of SS generals about the genocide, and two days later on the same topic to a larger gathering of the

Nazi bigwigs. He began by noting that this had become "the most difficult issue of my life":

> I want here to openly mention a very difficult chapter. Among us we can talk about it . . . we will never talk about it in public. What I mean is the evacuation, the extermination of the Jewish people. Most of you know what it means to [see] 100, 500 or a 1,000 dead bodies lying together. To have endured this, and, apart from exceptions due to human weakness, to have remained decent (*anständig*), has hardened us. This is a glorious chapter in our history, which will not be written now or in the future because we know how difficult it would have been if Jews had still been able to act as secret saboteurs, agitators, and rabble-rousers (*Hetzer*) while cities are being bombed, people are [heavily] burdened and subjected to wartime deprivations. Had we still had this corroding plague in our body politic, we would not have been able to endure the burdens of the fourth year of war and perhaps the fifth or sixth. . . . We would probably have been in the situation of 1916/17 when the Jews were still members of the German people.

Himmler elaborated further:

> The question arose: what to do with the women and children? I decided to find a complete solution. I felt justified to exterminate not just the men, i.e., to kill them or let them die. . . . Our heartfelt feelings as Germans do not entitle us to allow vengeful and hate-filled [young Jews] to grow up . . . so that our children and grandchildren would have to struggle with them. . . . The difficult decision had to be made to let this people disappear from the earth. (International Military Tribunal, 145–146, 161–162)

He concluded:

> The Jewish question has been solved in Germany and in the main in the German occupied countries. This was done without any compromise as part of the struggle for the survival

> of our people and its blood. . . . I was fully convinced of its necessity. . . . In this conflict with Asia, we must cast aside and forget the old cherished rules of the game of past European wars. (Longerich, 2008, Himmler, 715)

In the spring of 1944, as defeat loomed, Himmler repeatedly reminded army generals about their complicity in the Holocaust. The Reichsführer-SS pointed out that the military had become an instrument to achieve the ideological goals of the regime, one of which was to murder Europe's Jews. If Germany lost the war, he said, the military would share in the responsibility for the genocide and not be able to claim that it didn't know. Himmler also repeated his point about the necessity to kill the women and children (715).

Jews were the principal targets of the Holocaust, but the Nazi zeal to purify Europe was by no means limited to them. About five million gentiles were killed in Germany and in occupied countries, especially non-Jewish Poles and Russians (*Untermenschen*—subhumans). The largest group consisted of about three million Soviet prisoners of war. Political commissars, Communist Party members, and Jews were shot immediately after capture. Most perished in POW camps from maltreatment, deliberate starvation, and untreated epidemics ("Documenting . . . the victims"). As Himmler put it in his 1943 speech:

> Whether 10,000 Russian females collapse from exhaustion when digging an anti-tank ditch is of interest to me only to the extent that the ditch is completed for Germany. . . . If someone objects that "I can't build an anti-tank ditch with children or women since they will die which is inhuman", the reply should be: "You are murdering your own blood, because if the ditch is not built, German soldiers will die'. . . . Our duty is to our people and our blood (International Military Tribunal).

A poem by Paul Celan, "Todesfuge" ("Deathfugue") captures what the genocide meant for the victims:

> Black milk of daybreak we drink it at evening
> we drink at midday and morning we drink it at night
> we drink and we drink
> we shovel a grave in the air where you won't lie too cramped

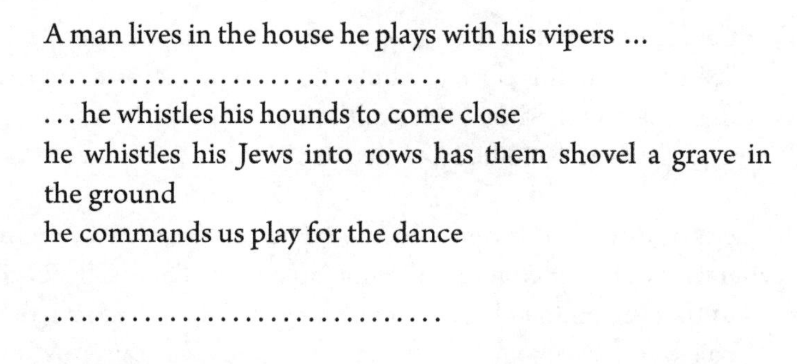

A man lives in the house he plays with his vipers ...

....

. . . he whistles his hounds to come close
he whistles his Jews into rows has them shovel a grave in the ground
he commands us play for the dance

....

He shouts jab this earth deeper you lot there you others sing up and play
he grabs for the rod in his belt he swings it his eyes are so blue . . . .
He shouts play death more sweetly this Death is a master from Deutschland

he shoots you with shot made of lead shoots you level and true

he plays with his vipers and daydreams der Tod ist ein Meister aus Deutschland.
(Felstiner, 31–32, excerpts)

CHAPTER 4

Our Family in Berlin During the Nazi Years

1933–1939

After the dissolution of the home collective, Paul and Johanna found a place to live in the rear building (*Hinterhof*) of an apartment complex, which was difficult to locate and was something of a refuge from harassment. For them this was "internal exile," a widely used term that signified the intent to live separately from the regime. They used this apartment for gatherings of like-minded friends, among them veterans and people the Nazis had imprisoned and then released. They held weekly evening discussions, sometimes on signs of resistance to and crises within the regime, but usually they listened to lectures on history, literature, religion, or philosophy. This became a way of upholding German cultural values in the face of Nazi lies and vulgarizations, which my sister rightly calls "evasive resistance" (information provided by Barbara Bernstein).

But as time passed, a good many of their friends stopped coming. One of them, a fellow-student, had kept in touch and complained about Nazi antisemitism. But when Paul and Johanna visited his apartment, his wife, having heard of a relative's affair with a *Mischling*, complained about "dirty Jews." Her husband berated her, but as Paul and Johanna left, they caught a glimpse of his SS uniform (*Dreams*, 166–7). Johanna thought that a good many highly educated young men joined the SS because it was an elite organization.

Paul's and Johanna's apartment turned out not to be all that safe from harassment. Antisemites discovered them and sent hate mail; one such letter calls Johanna a "Jewish sow" (letter, 1966). Persecutors pounded on their door and then disappeared. Friends stood guard.

Such events raise a fundamental question: Why didn't our parents try to emigrate before it was too late? After all, many German Jews were leaving Germany, and I got to know quite a few who taught in colleges and universities in this country. The major reason for staying was Paul's love for Germany and Johanna's attachment to the German language. Although Paul taught classes for prospective emigrants, he himself was too proud to leave, believing it was wrong to run away. He, like many German Jews, regarded the Nazis as un-German. In her 1966 letter to us, Johanna writes that Paul's

> greatest weakness, which you must know about, was undoubtedly his love for Germans and Germany, a childish love that prevented him from relying on his normal rational stance. In the final analysis, this is why he perished. In addition, his eagerness to learn about contemporary political developments often made him forget that he personally might be affected by what was happening. Add my fears of sprachlicher Entwurzelung [estrangement from her native language—T. B.] all this prevented our early emigration.

Johanna reports that early on Paul diagnosed the hatred towards defenseless Jews as deliberately organized in order to divert the angry unemployed masses from directing their hatred towards capitalists and the government: "We had of course learned about the terrible mistreatment of people in the concentration camps but thought of them as acts of individual sadists who were inspired by Nazi praise for brutality. No one, including we, could imagine what was to come." The couple thought that they could endure the hard times of Hitler's rule because the "Nazi nightmare will pass" (*Dreams*, 100). But after *Kristallnacht*, they finally decided to leave Germany.

In 1934, Johanna became pregnant with Barbara—and not by accident. "Their friends and relatives were aghast." What future would a half-Jew have in Germany as a second-class citizen, whom officials would blame if anything went awry. Paul responded "that this won't happen and his wife asked how he would prevent it" (104).

Johanna and Paul had by then befriended a Catholic prelate (*Domprobst*), Bernhard Lichtenberg, who prayed for inmates of concentration camps and "in a loud voice, for the persecuted Jews.... Lord, show mercy to them" (105). His Friday evening prayers could be heard outside his church and attracted an audience of listeners, our parents among them. Many were deeply moved and prayed with Lichtenberg. But members of the SA and SS who heard him became enraged by his prayers for the Jews. In *Dreams*, Johanna writes:

> Wasn't it right to go after Jews? Hadn't Germans been taught during their religious instruction that Jews were the descendants of Christ's killers and therefore shared their guilt . . . many Catholics were devoted nationalists; it was common for priests to voice their love for the fatherland and to support rearmament (105).

Lichtenberg's courage deeply impressed our parents. They feared that he risked arrest, but he didn't think he was in danger. He said that if he were imprisoned, "there's nothing to be done" and continued to pray for the persecuted (137). Lichtenberg baptized Barbara and told Johanna that the child would be protected by the Church. Barbara's certificate of baptism states that Paul is Jewish and Johanna a Protestant, indicating that she had not converted to Catholicism. Perhaps she was aware of her husband's biting critique of a papal encyclical which reiterated the Church's orthodox stance on marriage and the family in a 1931 issue of the *Socialist Young Workers Journal*. The prelate was later arrested and died on a transport to Dachau concentration camp (see later in this chapter).

In order to get some relief from the pressures to which they were subjected, Johanna and Barbara went to a small, isolated hotel outside of Berlin run by members of a Christian sect that still welcomed Jewish guests. At dinner one evening, Johanna noticed a younger man who was said to be hard of hearing, but who was actually listening, when someone made a remark about a new *Verordnung* (decree) on hotels and inns. Two days later, a pair of Gestapo agents burst into the house and arrested an elderly woman, demanding to know where her husband was. When the innkeeper responded that she didn't know, one of the agents got angry: "You must know that Jews are forbidden to sleep in hotels" (122). Johanna and the baby immediately left to stay with friends until she learned that it was safe to return home.

And then another child was born. I, too, was a product of an intended pregnancy, and Lichtenberg also baptized me. I was not circumcised, a practice which in Germany was mainly performed on Jews, and so I lack this affirmation of membership in the Jewish community, but this no doubt enabled me to survive. My birth was difficult for my parents. They went to a clinic, but the nurses were nasty. The obstetrician was a repellent and inebriated Nazi who shouted, "Let the woman come," instead of using the polite expression, "Let the gracious lady come." Offended, Paul took his wife to a Catholic hospital, which accepted the couple, even though its obstetric wards were overcrowded, since Germans were supposed to have lots of children for their Führer. After my birth, my father had to go to a police station to register my existence. There he was made to stand at the entrance and loudly announce, "I am the Jew, Paul Bernstein," whereupon everybody started to laugh (letter, 1966).

After my birth, one of Johanna's aunts, a fervent Nazi, came to visit. Having warned her niece not to get involved with Jews, she asked: "Is your husband home? He is not worth meeting. I only want to see how you are. Does he mistreat you? I hear you have children by him." Accustomed to friendly reactions when visitors saw the children, Johanna took her to their room. She watched expectantly as the aunt looked hard at Barbara, who was playing while I slept. The aunt's face remained immobile, as if frozen. Johanna shuddered. Breathing heavily and full of fear, she pushed the aunt out of the room, whereupon the aunt said:

> "One couldn't as yet tell anything about the children. They still had baby blond hair and their skulls were underdeveloped. As most often happens, in a few years the bad race will then come to dominate." "Get out," Johanna hissed. The aunt stared at her and left, livid with anger. On the stairway, she encountered Paul, who was preoccupied with his own thoughts and didn't recognize her. She spat in his face: "You have my niece on your conscience, you, you Jew" (*Dreams*, 142–3).

Our mother suffered a severe breakdown in late 1937. Barbara told me that it was caused not only by these political pressures but also by "the overwhelming drudgery of daily housework." Diapers had to be washed by hand but, unlike most German men at the time, Paul took part in this task (information provided by Barbara Bernstein).

Prelate Lichtenberg arranged for Johanna to recuperate in a cloister, and for us to go to a Catholic children's home, where we spent six weeks. Barbara wrote that

> when we arrived, I was fast asleep and the nuns cooed and clucked over me but tied me to a play horse. Our parents left abruptly and weren't allowed to visit us. [During that era, pediatricians recommended that children would adapt more easily if they realized that their parents would not come back—T. B.]. No one explained to me why our parents had abandoned us. Sad and lonely, I lost appetite, and when the nuns forced me to swallow lettuce leaves, I almost choked. I had trouble sleeping because the room was brightly lit and the other children were noisy.

Johanna later told her that when she and Paul came to bring us home, they were shocked by how much weight Barbara had lost.

In 1938, someone stole some money from Johanna. Assuming remnants of the rule of law remained, Paul insisted that Johanna complain to the police. She was summoned to police headquarters, where an official screamed at her: "How dare you, the wife of a Jew, accuse an Aryan of a crime?" (information provided by our mother).

Between 1933 and 1939, the family lived by pawning the very substantial collection of jewelry and other valuables left by Paul's mother and aunt and by Johanna's father. Because he was Jewish, he was paid little for the jewels. After *Kristallnacht*, Gestapo agents searched their apartment and confiscated the remaining jewelry as part of the one-billion-mark fine imposed on Jews.

At one point, Paul was assigned by the state employment office to a temporary road construction job. He was paid less than his Aryan coworkers, but the work did sustain the family for two to three months. A friend let Paul work in his law office, but he had to leave because the cleaning woman threatened to report his presence. He also had periodic part-time jobs such as sewing gloves and jackets and clipping newspaper articles but these sporadic earnings simply could not support a family of four.

In the spring of 1939, the family ran out of money. Johanna kept looking for work. Her poor health made it impossible to do physical labor, so she looked for entry-level jobs as an office stenographer. Invariably, she was turned down because of her husband's race. Finally, a publishing house hired her on condition that she divorce Paul. The boss sympathized with her plight and urged her to do so, saying it would be only a formality. The divorce was a desperate act which they discussed with Prelate Lichtenberg. Although the

Catholic Church strongly opposed divorce, Lichtenberg told them that in the eyes of the Church, they still would be married and that after the war he would reformalize the marriage. He advised Paul that in order to convince the court to grant a divorce, he would have to lie and confess to adultery, which he did. Although the court was supposed to appoint a guardian for Barbara and me, Johanna, who did not have to appear in court, was awarded custody. The court noted that we were being raised as Catholics. By the time the divorce was legal, however, the publishing job had disappeared. Paul and Johanna then decided that she and us would move to Leipzig, her hometown, hoping that she might find a job there, which indeed was the case (see Chapter 5).

Divorce meant that any relations between the two would be regarded as *Rassenschande* (race defilement) and lead to severe punishment. Nevertheless, they decided to meet secretly as often as possible. After the war, our mother learned that had they stayed married, Paul might well have survived. Mixed couples were privileged and a good many did see liberation. And what they did not and could not have anticipated was that during the Holocaust, a divorce meant that the Jewish partner could be deported.

I was too young to remember our life in Berlin. *Dreams* suggests, however, that the turmoil in the family did have an impact on me. The following scene took place in September 1939, when Barbara was already in Leipzig and I was about to go there, accompanied by Oma, our step grandmother:

> On another day, mother's little boy is standing stiff as a rod in the middle of a sidewalk. People have to go around him, which they do with amused smiles. She squats in front of him and quietly tries talking to him. Oma is impatient. She puts the suitcase down and looks at her watch. "We'll miss the train, pick the boy up." But as much as he likes to be carried, today he senses that something uncanny is going on, which causes him to be afraid. Not even a train trip can excite him. He doesn't want to go on the train with a woman whom he scarcely knows. He wants to go back to his room and eat the apple which he had left there.
>
> The previous week had been very hard for him. Incomprehensible changes were taking place. Father only comes for an occasional quick and furtive visit. Movers take furniture away; boxes filled with books lie on the floor. His

> mother doesn't sing him to sleep. Her eyes are full of tears and she has wrapped a thick scarf around her neck. Her voice is hoarse as she sniffles and is afraid to kiss him (*Dreams*, 198).

Paul and Johanna sought to leave Germany after *Kristallnacht.* The main obstacle to emigration was their near destitution. Paul asked a wealthy cousin, Toni Witkowski, for the money they needed to leave, but she refused, only to see her own property confiscated. Alice Hanson Cook provided the required affidavit for a visa which entailed signing a pledge to support our family so that we would not have to depend on public welfare. The affidavit did arrive, but they were unable to emigrate. US consulates were overrun by desperate applicants and our family's number on the US quota list for German immigrants was very low. The delay meant that their hopes were dashed because of the outbreak of WWII in September 1939 and the closing of the borders (Landesarchiv-Berlin).

Paul tried to emigrate to Sweden. He learned how to electroplate (*Galvanik*) metal objects in order to find employment there. Barbara told me that acquiring this skill delayed his emigration. He thought he would need a year to save enough money to bring his family to Sweden. Prelate Lichtenberg offered to do all he could to enable our mother and us to leave. "In 1938 he was put in charge of the relief office of the Berlin episcopate, which assisted many Catholics of Jewish descent in emigrating from the Third Reich" (Wikipedia, "Bernhard Lichtenberg").

The Prelate also informed our parents about the relief office's funds that could be used to help Catholic children of mixed marriages to emigrate. Again, the war intervened although some Jews did manage to get out before October 1941 when Jewish emigration was banned altogether.

Paul's older brother, Richard, also sought belatedly to leave Germany. As noted in Chapter 2, he knew of an uncle, Adolf Bernstein, who had settled in the US in the 1890s. (It is not clear what Paul knew about this relative). When we met Adolf's granddaughter, Emily Berleth, in 2013, she gave us the letters that Richard had written between February 1939 and November 1940 which convey his growing desperation. He asks for an affidavit of support. He apologizes for the imposition, but insists that he is self-reliant, well acquainted with business, and that he will not need to ask for money. He received the affidavit, but the US consulate failed to issue the visa.

Prelate Lichtenberg's oppositional activities against the Nazis went far beyond the assistance that he gave to our family. Between 1933 and his arrest in 1941, he persisted in praying for the persecuted Jews. During *Kristallnacht* he told members of the Cathedral of St. Hedwig, "The synagogue outside is burning, and that is also a house of God" (Wikipedia, "Bernhard Lichtenberg"). He protested to high-ranking officials about the cruelties perpetrated in a concentration camp, and in 1941 wrote a letter to the minister of public health, Leonard Conti, castigating him for the murder of mentally ill patients:

> I, as a human being, a Christian, and a German, demand of you, Chief Physician of the Reich, that you answer for the crimes that have been perpetrated at your bidding . . . and which will call forth the vengeance of the Lord on the heads of the German people.

Protests by some "highly admired bishops" and by the public caused enough concern to prompt the Nazi authorities to terminate the euthanasia program. When the deportations began, Lichtenberg requested permission to accompany Jews in order to comfort them. Two students denounced him, and he was arrested in October 1941 and "sentenced to two years in state prison for violation of the Pulpit Law and Treachery Act of 1934." After his release, the Gestapo rearrested him in 1943, viewing him as "incorrigible." He died on the way to Dachau concentration camp. In 1996, he was beatified by Pope John Paul II, and in 2004 recognized by Israel's Yad Vashem as Righteous Among the Nations (ibid).

Paul Alone in Berlin, 1939–1944

Our father rejoined the Jewish community, exclaiming in mock horror: "Die haben mich zu den Juden geschmissen" (the Nazis have thrown me to the Jews). In 1940, five-year-old Barbara traveled alone by train to Berlin, where her father met her at the station and took her home to his room in a *Judenhaus*. Barbara vividly remembers the details:

> His home was a narrow attic with a low, slanted roof rising from the floor, just enough space for a bed underneath it, a little cabinet at the foot-end, a stand with a wash-basin, a pitcher on the floor . . . with a small window, the only source

> of light and ventilation. . . . We slept, with a gap between our backs. . . . Every morning . . . he gave me a teaspoonful of marmalade.

Because she snored, Paul moved the bed into the small hallway directly under the window, for more air, but she continued to snore and so he took her to a clinic where her tonsils were "capped":

> We entered a large room with a wide circle of chairs, each taken by a person with a child. Paul sat down with me on his lap. . . . [A] doctor went around, a nurse by his side carried a big tray of gleaming instruments which I admired. The children were given a [local] anesthetic: I opened my mouth as told and held still while I heard cracking and crunching as he worked, but it didn't hurt, I was unfazed by the blood spilling into a bowl. I felt easy and safe on my father's lap.

When all the kids had been treated, the parents stood up, relieved, talking with one another and the doctor. . . . Paul gave me a look and quietly left with me. (I didn't know then that crowds could turn dangerous) . . . We will never know how much diplomacy or persuasion Paul had to expend to get me admitted.
The surgery succeeded in ending her snoring.

> Later, they went to another building:
> Paul took me to another clinic in a big house and told her to wait on the stairs. A tall door opened to a hall inside with a huge upholstered chair, Paul sat down on it, a doctor in a white coat appeared, and the door was gently closed. I wasn't told at the time that this was certainly one of the Jewish dentists and doctors who were now forbidden to treat Aryans.

Barbara and her father visited a Jewish retraining facility where Paul taught:

> The room . . . had a wonderful smell of fresh-cut wood, tables with tools . . . curls of cut wood and sawdust everywhere, and friendly young men looking down at me, talking. . . .

> Another day I met "Tante Bab" [Aunt Bab] smiling at me and I smiled back at her. She was short, her face was close to me—the next time I saw her, she gave me a white dress . . . that fitted perfectly (without her taking my measurements). . . . [W]e also met Walter Raue, a family friend. [His son, Andreas, played with us in Leipzig—T. B.]. These meetings took place on the streets, it was warm and sunny—only in retrospect was it obvious to me that Paul's place was too small to entertain guests. (Information provided by Barbara Bernstein)

According to Johanna, Paul was assigned to forced labor at the Siemens Company in Berlin. However, in the 1990s, this firm informed me that Paul was not listed in their archive. His 1944 property declaration stated that he worked for a trash collection firm, which presumably served Siemens. His job was to clean sewers, toilets, and carry coal and trash. The work was strenuous, dirty, and exhausting, and Jews received only 30–50% of the rations allocated to Aryans. During their last meeting in Berlin in 1943, he "laughed bitterly" when Johanna, shocked by his "sunken eyes, worn-out face, and bruised hands" asked about his ten-hour work day:

> I feel anger and fury. I feel humiliated. Within the plant area, we are not allowed to use the sidewalks for those are only for the master race but not for their slaves who do the dirty work. And they expect gratitude. It is a privilege to be allowed to labor here. And if you don't hustle, they'll deport you (*Dreams*, 222).

After the war, Johanna told Barbara that some of Paul's friends had offered to hide him. The idea was that he would stay in one apartment and then move on to another so that he could avoid having to register with the police. Paul refused the offer, not wanting to endanger his prospective hosts. A good many Jews, however, did rely on such help. They were called "U-Boats" (submarines). Many were caught but others survived until liberation.

In March 1943, Paul was ordered to prepare for his "evacuation" (one of several euphemisms for deportation). His sister-in-law, Gertrude, Richard's ex-wife, informed Johanna, who immediately went to Berlin with the tacit permission of her workplace bosses. With Gertrude's help and that of some friends, she wrote letters to Gestapo headquarters and other agencies, invoking Paul's wartime wounds and decorations. As proof that he had been providing obligatory child support, she showed receipts for the monthly money orders for forty to fifty Reichsmarks that he had sent to Leipzig, out of his meager wage of 136–160 Reichsmarks. Paul had told her to save the receipts to prevent deportation, "otherwise we will never see each other again." Johanna succeeded in speaking to a Nazi official, who told her that Paul's "evacuation" would be delayed. Not knowing what to believe, she wandered around Berlin in tears, finally ending up in Gertrude's apartment, where she found Paul. He had been on a deportation train when a loudspeaker had suddenly announced: "Paul Bernstein, *raus*" (out; 1966 letter.) Yad Vashem, Israel's Holocaust memorial, sent me an entry from a Gestapo file that states that he was on the "fourth enlarged transport of the aged" to an "unknown destination."

Paul sent a last letter to the family in Leipzig dated December 19, 1943:

> Dear Hanni [Johanna's shortened name], Oma, Baerbel, Thomas: This time I can only send you Christmas greetings through the mail. I feel very sorry that I can't come for a visit. But there is a war on, and many daddies can't visit their children and celebrate Christmas with them. Unfortunately, I can't send you any packages, so you will have to be a bit patient. As soon as packages can be sent, I will send you some things with which to play, and hopefully you'll have fun with them and will be happy even though they will arrive later. Mommy wrote that your books all burned up [in an air raid on December 4, 1943]. I am sending you some books and hope that they will still arrive more or less on time. I only got them just now. So, I wish that all of you can spend the [Christmas] holidays in peace and quiet, and that you'll have a good time despite all the troubles and that you will also think of your Dati [daddy] who greets you with all his heart.

Deaths in the Bernstein Family During the Holocaust

The first to die was Toni Witkowski, Isidor's wealthy cousin, who had refused to provide funds for our emigration. As neighbors reported after the war, Toni had to sit on a park bench painted yellow, "nur für Juden" (only for Jews), and during air raids was separated from Aryans in the shelter. On December 18, 1941, at age sixty-two, she took her life to evade her impending deportation. For the same reason, in January 1943 another Witkowski relative, Herta, forty-seven, and her husband, Sigismund, emulated Toni by committing suicide (information provided by Amelie Döge).

Johanna wrote about another family, including a young woman, a cousin of Paul's, whom she describes as very sensitive and well educated. After they were deported, she surmised that they perished during the Holocaust together with her family (*Dreams*, 274). The fate of Tante Bab, who had made a dress for Barbara, is not known. No doubt she was also murdered.

In the immediate Bernstein family, Paul's aunt Regina Herzberg died in 1942, Uncle Richard in 1943, and our father in 1944. Regina had a better feel for what the future held than did our parents, remarking at some point in the late 1930s that "they [the Nazis] will do us all in" (die bringen uns alle um). Paul responded by saying, "You speak of extermination, but how do you imagine it? Yes, individuals like you and me but (killing) millions is not technically feasible, possible only in open battle. These are verbal excesses" (*Dreams*, 184). Paul probably drew on memories of his frontline service in WWI, during which large numbers of soldiers were killed or injured by gas warfare. By 1942 or so, he had heard rumors about extermination. In her 1966 letter to Barbara and me, our mother writes that "he recognized only belatedly that in the German character (*Wesen*), as it had developed historically, there was the latent possibility of organized genocide."

Regina lived in a Jewish home for the aged in Berlin, whose patients were deported on June 9, 1942, to the Theresienstadt Ghetto. Before her deportation, she had to fill out a detailed property declaration (*Vermögensklärung*), which I found in an archive in 2010, together with those of Richard and Paul. These questionnaires demanded information about forced labor (*Dienstverpflichtung*—duty to serve), taxes owed, assets and belongings down to underwear. After Jews had been collected at their deportation sites, the Gestapo gave them a notarized receipt stating that their property was now the possession of the German Reich, in compliance with a decree passed on July 14, 1933, the Gesetz über die Einziehung volks- und staatsfeindlichen Vermögens (Law on the Confiscation of Property of the People and State) (Brandenburgisches Landeshauptsarchiv).

After the transports left, officials of the Ministry of Finance conducted extensive investigations to determine whether all property had in fact been taken, which often required prolonged correspondence with banks and real estate firms—an example of the complicity of the German state bureaucracy in the Nazi terror. Regina's property form was very short, since she had nothing, but this did not prevent further inquiries. A document dated March 12, 1945, two months before Germany's surrender, stated that there was in fact no property that could be seized (Vermögensverwertungsstelle—Office for Property Utilization; Berlin-Brandenburg Landeshauptarchiv).

Theresienstadt was a "privileged" ghetto set up in 1941 for the elderly, members of the Jewish cultural elite, and decorated and/or wounded Jewish WWI veterans. Under SS supervision, an Ältestenrat (Council of Elders) administered the camp, and inmates were able to maintain an improvised but high-quality cultural life that provided a respite from the prevailing misery. An attached facility, known as the "Little Fortress," was a small concentration camp in which the brutal practices of such camps were in force. Some offending ghetto inmates were executed there. Dorothy Solinger and I visited both the ghetto and the Little Fortress in July 2004.

In 1944, the Nazis made a film about Theresienstadt entitled *Der Fuehrer schenkt den Juden eine Stadt* (*The Führer Gives a City to the Jews*), which I have seen. It depicts inmates as workers, gardeners, musicians, and lecturers, that is, as normal people rather than despised parasites. This film was apparently not shown in Germany because it contradicted Nazi beliefs about Jews and also because Theresienstadt had not been bombed, unlike most German cities, which the authorities thought might cause popular resentment. Evidently, the film was intended to curry favor with the Allies, who by then had learned about the Holocaust.

The reality was that about 140,000 people were sent to this ghetto. By May 1945, 33,000 had died in Theresienstadt, mostly of epidemics, common diseases of old age but aggravated by overcrowding, malnourishment, lack of medicines, and mistreatment. The three and a half months that Regina was held there were particularly awful. About 18,000 of the 47,000 inmates then in the ghetto perished. The Council of Elders allocated more rations to children in the hope of improving their chances for survival. Old people suffered greatly, and there are pathetic descriptions of them scrounging garbage cans. Regina died on October 13, 1942 at age seventy-nine. Her death certificate states that she had dementia and died of heart failure.

More than half the inmates—86,934—were deported to the eastern killing centers, of whom only 2,971 survived. Inmates over sixty-five were at first exempted from deportation. At the end of 1942, this concession was abrogated until autumn 1944, when it was reinstated. Fundamentally,

Theresienstadt was a transit camp to the death camps (Lederer, 25 and other pages).

Before their divorce, Uncle Richard signed over his property to his Aryan wife, who then reverted to the use of her maiden name, Schroen. As in our parents' case, divorce meant the loss of the privileged status of mixed couples. When Richard was about to be deported in February 1943, Gertrude appealed to the Gestapo for his release. They mockingly asked why she was worried about him. After all, she'd got his money, hadn't she?

From early 1942, Richard had a room in a *Judenhaus* for which he paid forty Reichsmarks per month. His ex-wife donated some dishware and furniture. According to his property declaration, he had some cash, a winter and summer coat, three shirts, and one pair of shoes. Although he had signed over his real holdings to his wife, he was still listed as the owner of two houses, one of which had been destroyed in an air raid and the other one of which was confiscated. He listed his occupation as assistant locksmith (*Hilfsschlosser*) and was paid an hourly wage of three-fourths of a mark.

As in Aunt Regina's case, the Ministry of Finance carried out a lengthy investigation to ascertain whether he still owed taxes, had money in his bank and postal savings accounts, and whether the Ministry could get hold of the properties now owned by his ex-wife. One issue that required correspondence was that ten Reichsmarks were missing from one of his accounts.

Uncle Richard's deportation train left Berlin on March 3, 1943, bound directly for Auschwitz. He was weakened by forced labor and meager rations, and I surmise he was sent to a gas chamber directly from the railroad ramp without being admitted to the camp. Had he entered the camp, he would have received a number tattooed on his lower arm, leaving a record. In 1998, the Auschwitz-Birkenau Museum wrote to me that records for both Richard and Paul could not be found.

Paul's temporary reprieve ended on January 21, 1944, when he was sent to Theresienstadt. The "Transportliste" names 19 Jews, among them our father, who had been married to Aryan spouses and were deported because they had divorced them and thus were no long entitled to exemptions from deportation ("nicht mehr bestehende privilegierte Mischehe," no longer existing mixed marriage). These individuals came from various German cities, indicating that they were part of a nationwide round-up.

> *Vermögenserklärung* (Property Declaration), January 19, 1944 (excerpts from Paul Bernstein's questionnaire)
>
> Previous occupation: white-collar worker. Jew? Yes.
>
> Last occupation: worker at Trash Collection Firm. Wage: 35–40 marks per week.
>
> Residence: furnished room in an apartment owned by a Jewish woman. Rent, 25 marks per month.
>
> Wife, Aryan
>
> Children: Renate Bernstein (Barbara's middle name), May 31, 1935.
> Thomas Bernstein, April 11, 1937.
> Obligatory child support, 40–50 marks per month.
>
> I emphatically declare that the answers to the questionnaire are accurate to the best of my knowledge.
>
> *Verfügung* (order) by Secret State Police, Berlin. In compliance with the law authorizing confiscation of the property of enemies of the people and state, Bernstein's property is hereby confiscated for the benefit of the German Reich.
>
> This notarized document was handed to Paul Israel Bernstein at the Grosse Hamburger Strasse, Berlin (a collection site for deportees). Signed by a court bailiff on behalf of the Secret State Police, Berlin.

Johanna got a telegram from an acquaintance who had lived in Paul's *Judenhaus*, hinting that Paul was being deported. Johanna went immediately to Berlin to remonstrate, but Paul was already gone. She succeeded in obtaining the address of Ghetto Theresienstadt. As described in Chapter 5, we were then hiding in a village in the Sudetenland, not too distant from the ghetto, and our mother decided to try to see him. In a letter she sent to Alice Hanson Cook in July 1947, she writes about her effort to do so: "I illegally crossed the border to the Czech Protectorate. Because of the extremely cold winter, I was terribly worried about his fragile health. He had endured several years of forced labor with totally inadequate rations and had to work hard doing menial tasks."

She caught a glimpse of some wretched-looking inmates, but was sharply rebuffed by SS guards who barked: "You Jewish sow, you want to end up in this place? Get out of here." Two armed guards escorted her to the railroad station, raging against the so-called privileges enjoyed by Jews in the ghetto. "She felt powerless love, anger, and hate" (*Dreams*, 284). On the return trip to Leipzig, she "overheard SS men talking about how the bodies of concentration camp inmates were boiled down into soap."

Johanna learned that relatives were allowed to send a monthly five hundred gram package, and in March, 1944, she began to post packages of food and clothing. Months later, in July, she received her first acknowledgement from her husband in the form of a printed postcard signed with the message, "I am well." In her letter to Alice, she writes: "This was of course enormously encouraging and I hoped he would endure." Johanna kept sending packages, but further acknowledgments came only in August and September. Despite inquiries, we have no information on how Paul fared during his eight months in Theresienstadt.

Geheran, who relies heavily on the diaries of incarcerated veterans, quotes a Danish survivor:

> This is possibly the greatest shame for the Nazis, that these people who sacrificed their limbs for Germany ... were dragged into this misery. A number of them do not have arms, and others only one, one-and-a half, or three-quarters of a leg. The completely legless do not collect their rations on their own—one only sees them hobble about on their stumps in the dirty, ground-floor rooms, using only the strength of their arms, like small kangaroos, not like humans. The ones who have it worst off are those lost their eyes; they have to collect their rations by themselves, and in their blindness, are almost always tricked by the cooks.

A diary by a Czech veteran who was imprisoned in the Small Fortress for minor offenses:

> The Jewish police did not want to beat him. He was wounded in the war, they said. He lost his arm for Germany. "Indeed," replied the German commandant, "he must get 25 lashes."
>
> In the space of eight months from July 1943 to March 1944, the Ghetto Health Department recorded that 17 percent of the overall veteran population perished (186–189).

At the same time, Geheran found that the status of veterans did matter. "It is conceivable that the mortality rate among war invalids would have been even higher if it had not been for the additional ration allotments." He reiterates his argument that veteran maintained "their psychological connections to their former status as frontline fighters" and memories of their heroism and ability to withstand the deprivations of trench warfare, thereby preserving their sense of honor in face of Nazi humiliation and cruel mistreatment. Also, wounded and decorated veterans were "officially exempt from the deportations" to the death camps until September 1944 (189–90).

In mid-May, 1944, a census of Theresienstadt listed inmates whose protected status exempted them from deportation. Among them were 915 war invalids together with 800 family members and 1,614 decorated veterans with 1,418 family members. Also included were 1,524 *Mischlinge* with 590 family members and 1,954 partners in mixed marriages with 38 family members. A rough estimate is that altogether 6,500 inmates were protected by the Jewish administration (Lederer, 28).

Between May 18 and September 27, 1944 there were no transports from Theresienstadt to Auschwitz, whose killers were too busy murdering Hungary's Jews. Transports to Auschwitz resumed on September 28 and ended on October 28, 1944. To deceive inmates about their true intent, the SS told the Jewish administration that males born between 1889 and 1928 would be put to work at other locations. In all, 18,402 prisoners were deported to Auschwitz, including members of the Council of Elders. In the frenzied drive to assemble them, some *Mischlinge* were included. Only 1,496 survived (Lederer, 156).

Veterans were deported because they were now regarded as "grave security risks." Himmler had learned of an "imminent and coordinated" uprising by Cech resistance groups that would very likely take place in September 1944, which could free Theresienstadt's inmates and enable veterans with combat experience to join them. A recent uprising in Slovakia confirmed the threat, when partisans liberated Jews, many of whom joined in the fight against the German occupiers (Geheran, 200). Himmler told his subordinates in Prague to prepare for this critical event, adding: "We are clear about the measures" to be taken (Karny). Among the veterans, six hundred war invalids were sent, of whom 175 survived (202).

Paul was on the second transport that left on September 29, 1944, with 1,500 Jews, arriving at Auschwitz on October 1. Half of them were gassed on arrival, most likely including our father, who was weakened from forced labor and malnutrition. This is how his "fatherland" thanked him for his service in WWI.

CHAPTER 5

Leipzig, 1939–1945

Our Mother, Step-Grandmother, Barbara and Thomas

Barbara and I moved to Leipzig in early September 1939 to live with Oma. Johanna lived separately in a small apartment in another part of town, perhaps for reasons of space, or more likely, because of their mutual dislike. Accompanied by Oma, I left Berlin in September. Germany had just invaded Poland. I learned later that a banner displayed on a train read: "Jetzt fahren wir nach Polen um die Juden zu versohlen" (Now we are going to Poland in order to beat up the Jews). I am told that there were a lot of soldiers on our train who joked and played with me. But I must have been rather morose. When we arrived at Oma's apartment, I found my sister, who had left Berlin earlier, and I smiled happily on seeing her.

In 1940, our mother got a job with a steel wholesale company, C. F. Weithas. The director and a manager were not Nazis and were protective of her. Johanna confided in her boss, who regarded the Nazis as rowdies. A sympathetic employee helped her to find a place for Paul's visits. She failed as a stenographer, but was transferred to the sales department as a business correspondent, replacing a man who had been drafted. She had to learn the basics of sales and how to correspond with other firms, and she did well at these tasks, to her surprise. But many in the firm were suspicious, especially since she didn't raise her arm in the Hitler salute during assemblies.

In the early 1940s, I became very attached to Oma, who really cared for me. I dimly recall that she didn't get angry when I wet the bed or threw temper tantrums. She gave me a wooden hammer with which to hit a small bench—I presume as an outlet for my feelings. After we were bombed out in December of 1943 and had to move, I became more distant from her. In sharp contrast, Oma instantly disliked Barbara, perhaps repeating her years of tension with our mother. Barbara recalls that Oma was "cold, never hugged her, or showed any affection," and spanked her. She made her do chores, like dusting, drying dishes, and shining shoes, whereas I could play, which made her jealous. Her life with Oma was painful. She found some relief by being as independent as possible, reading, drawing, and making things. She was very happy when she was able to visit our mother, who was very busy at work (information provided by Barbara Bernstein).

I have no concrete memories of our father's visits to Leipzig at Christmas in 1939, 1940, and 1941, which, I was told later, were wonderful occasions for us. Barbara recalls that he performed a puppet show, which we loved. I learned after the war that during one visit I put a tin soldier in his pocket and that this was very moving. I have a shadowy image (or perhaps I was told later) that when I stuck a rusty nail into my thumb in Oma's garden, my father sucked the cut to staunch the bleeding.

During one of these visits, Oma, who gossiped thoughtlessly, told a neighbor that Paul was visiting. This neighbor went to the police, complaining how intolerable it was for a Jew to be staying there. The police arrived. Paul insisted, in vain, that he had the legal right to see his children. He was detained for a night and was put on a morning train back to Berlin. Oma wailed at this humiliation. The person who denounced our father evidently put up with the presence of two half-Jewish children.

Paul's Last Visit to Leipzig Followed by Johanna's Gestapo Interrogation

A Nazi secretary at Johanna's firm who caught a glimpse of the couple denounced her, and she was ordered to report to the Gestapo, an ordeal that she vividly describes in *Dreams*:

> She entered her interrogator's office. He told her, "Setz dich" (sit down, using the intimate Du rather than the polite Sie). He was taken aback by her Aryan good looks. Looking at her eyes, blond hair, and skin color, he said, "I had imagined that you wouldn't look so 'Nordic'. A woman like you and a Jew. You should be spanked." He leafed through her file saying, "You are divorced and weren't blamed. Yes or No?" Johanna, speaking hesitantly, said, "If I say yes, do you then conclude that my husband was guilty? He didn't do anything wrong."

> He replied, in a mocking tone, "Your husband pled guilty to a big marital offense, his Jewish betrayal, his infidelity." J. then explained that "I wasn't at the divorce court."
>
> Her inquisitor now adopted a milder tone. "Your absence is a good sign, indicating that you couldn't stand him even in the courtroom. You read the judgment and yet you maintain that your husband was innocent even though he admitted his guilt. Does this mean that he lied to the court? J. protested, "no, no." He gloated over her fear. She recalls sitting there, seemingly contrite and full of misery, suppressing her intense anger. The Gestapo official said, "How could you have married him? Were his riches so important to you?" But he didn't insist that she provide a written statement about Paul's lie.
>
> "So, you recognize that your relations with a Jew were contemptible. Despite this you have been meeting him. Don't lie, you were observed." J.: "He wanted to see his children who live with me." "So, they live with you, perhaps not for long." With that our mother almost fainted. . . . "If you are caught again with a Jew, you'll be sent to a home. Racial defilement is a serious crime against German blood." Then he gave her "advice" with regard to the children. "They must no longer see their father. He must not influence them. Of course, this won't improve the bad blood that they inherited from him." J. tried but couldn't cry. Then she saw that for some reason, her interrogator seemed moved by her. After a dozen more admonitions and threats, he let her go. He also did not do anything about the children or Paul. (Dreams, 210)

After this interview, the couple met only in Berlin. Herr Weithas superiors tacitly covered for her absences.

Barbara and I as *Mischlinge*. Flight to the Sudetenland in Early 1944

A rule stipulated that half-Jews could go to elementary school, but no further. But this privilege did not prevent half-Jews from being singled out in some way or other. Barbara experienced several hurtful incidents. When she raised her hand to respond to a teacher's questions, she was ignored. When a class photo was about to be taken, a teacher told her, "You can go" or "We don't need you here." Barbara told her mother about these incidents. Johanna was shocked, but had to minimize her reactions because she was afraid that my sister might tell her fellow pupils, so she could not explain to Barbara why she was being singled out. Also, Johanna never told us about Jewish customs, about which she knew a great deal, to avoid arousing suspicion.

After I turned six in 1943, Oma went to the principal of a nearby elementary school to enroll me. He admitted me, perhaps because I didn't look Jewish and had been baptized. I'm told that I obeyed his command to say "Heil Hitler" and stand at attention. He must have concluded that my Aryan blood outweighed my Jewish blood, in contrast to what Johanna's aunt had predicted. I don't recall experiencing the kind of school incidents that so troubled Barbara. One that I do remember took place when an older boy in our neighborhood pointed at me, his hand mimicking a pistol, and said, "Your father is a Jew." I said "No." Probably a relative of the boy had talked about the killing of Jews.

Policy towards first-degree *Mischlinge* hardened in late 1943 and 1944. Now, adults were no longer allowed to work as individuals but were to be sent in groups to labor camps or to Theresienstadt. My mother and Barbara once walked by a guarded enclosure in which very unhappy looking people were sitting with suitcases. One whispered to her that they were half-Jews. Also at this time, a *Mischling* who worked at the firm suddenly disappeared. Johanna and some colleagues went to her apartment and found that it had been sealed by the Gestapo.

Johanna decided to flee. We first went to Machern, a village near Leipzig, where we stayed in a weekend cottage owned by Mr. Weiss of Johanna's firm. When he came to visit, Barbara and I stood on a table shouting, "Onkel Weiss." In Machern, Johanna didn't register with the police, as was required. We did go to school, but in the absence of an Aryan certificate, suspicions arose. And because a hunt was on for a Soviet spy and houses were being searched, our mother took us to a pastor in another town, recommended by a relative of Johanna's close friend, Gretel Weisske. Johanna had hoped to stay there for a few days, but the pastor was "very, very sorry, but his congregation would not have understood his hiding Jewish children" (*Dreams*, 64).

Our mother then took us on a long train trip to Moosdorf relatives in Nedowitz, a village in the Sudetenland, now a part of the Czech Republic. The journey required several changes of trains, and at one stop, Johanna overheard someone muttering about a passing train, "wieder ein Judenzug" (another Jew train), and walked quickly away.

When we arrived at the village, Johanna didn't tell her relatives the real reason why we had come, pretending that she feared air raids. Had the truth been discovered, our hosts would no doubt have been punished. Villagers thought that she was a war widow and was applying for a pension. After a major air raid at the end of February 1944, Johanna made a brief visit to Leipzig and found that our apartment house was still intact.

We stayed in Nedowitz until March and attended a one-room school in a neighboring village. Barbara and I had a good time, riding on a horse-drawn sleigh, playing around the house with farm animals, and jumping on a frozen dung heap. But when a Nazi became suspicious, Johanna took us to another village and then back to Leipzig, "hoping that in this last year of the war, the Nazis wouldn't worry about *Mischlinge*. . . . [Then] she heard again that *Mischlinge* were being taken away," but soon learned that only adults were being rounded up (1947 letter to Alice Cook).

In all her travels, Johanna managed to get by without a proper identity card, an extraordinary feat in a country at war. She had only a Leipzig *Wohnungschein* (residence permit). A real ID would have listed us children as half-Jewish, which could have brought danger. In this and other situations, she used her tactical skills, learning to lie when necessary. For instance, during the trip to the Sudetenland, when we stayed overnight in a hotel, she used a false ID number on the registration form. Johanna had great, often desperate courage, a point that Barbara emphasizes.

Johanna's friend Gretel, whom she knew from the youth movement of the 1920s, lived with us in 1944. Since Johanna had left her firm and was without an income, Gretel supported us. Johanna ran a risk by persuading her not to join the Nazi Party. Gretel's husband, Georg Weisske, applied to join the SS at a time when Germany's enormous initial victories persuaded a great many Germans that Hitler would soon rule all of Europe and that they had better get on board. He told Johanna he joined because he wanted to advance his career. Georg fell in love with her and hoped to marry her after divorcing Gretel. As part of that plan, he would claim both Barbara and me as his own, having ascertained that our blood group was the same as those of his own children. He was stationed in occupied Poland and told Johanna that he knew that all Jews would be killed and that Hitler was determined to extirpate anyone with even a trace of Jewish blood. Georg said his goal was to save us and didn't care that Paul would have to die: "No one can escape." He elaborated:

> You are full of bitterness [about Paul]. Don't you know that you are faced with an immense power with a will to exterminate and a thoroughly planned death strategy? Any reasonable individual must regard you as a fool, a damned idiot, if you don't accept my offer of marriage (246–7).

He went on:

> You still haven't grasped what I'm telling you. The law of nature is merciless. The strong devour the weak. . . . It demands that we take advantage of the right of the stronger; it makes no difference who has to perish . . . you will never see Paul again.
> I've been in the East for a long time and with my own eyes have seen what is happening to the Jews. . . . Believe me, no one can escape.

This greatly frightened our mother; she screamed and said: "no one has ever mentioned witnessing such events. So, death and murder are no longer rumors. Please, what did you see? Georg stared into space." Gretel mockingly said: "when crimes are ordered by high officials, they are indeed state secrets. The German man knows how to keep them. So, Georg, perhaps did you yourself participate"? Johanna repeated that she would never accept his marriage proposal. "It sounded so final that he had to accept her words, but wondered why women could be so unreasonable" (285). Georg and Gretel started to hit each other with their fists. I recall watching as they screamed at each other. Divorce followed.

My mother was afraid that if I knew the truth about my father, I might inadvertently reveal it, so she told me that he was at the front, and this is what I said to my schoolmates. She persuaded Barbara to lie about her racial status before her tenth birthday on May 31, 1945 because children were required to register for the lowest tier of the Nazi youth organization (288). Fortunately, Germany had already surrendered.

Johanna was under enormous strain worrying about Paul and us. A photo of her taken in 1944 clearly shows this. In her letter to Alice, she writes: "someone told the Gestapo that I still had relations with my husband and I was ready to flee again, but the charge was dropped since, verifiably, Paul was no longer in Germany." An incident in 1944 illustrates the tension which Johanna experienced. Gretel's son, Peter, who lived with us, chronically wet his bed. Gretel and Johanna had to wash the sheets every day, a cumbersome task in the absence of washing machines. This so aggravated Johanna that she took a broom and beat him, which was totally out of character, but it did stop the bed-wetting.

The attempted assassination of Hitler on July 20, 1944, deeply shocked Johanna and, of course, aroused hope that her husband might return. When these hopes were dashed, her upbeat mood changed into "deep resignation." But people grumbled. She overheard neighbors who had never criticized their Führer now cursing him. A war-wounded worker was not denounced for collecting money to help Russian, Polish, and Jewish forced laborers, who had only bread to eat and wore torn clothes (287–8).

Air Raids, 1943–1945

Leipzig was not seriously bombed until December 4, 1943, when 267 British bombers raided the city in what was said to be a medium to heavy attack, killing 1,182 persons (Horn). When Allied air fleets crossed into Germany, a radio announcement alerted the public with a message that stuck in my head: "Achtung! Achtung! Anglo-Amerikanische Bomberverbaende in Richtung auf Hannover-Braunschweig" (Attention! Attention! Anglo-American bomber formations flying towards these two cities in northwestern Germany). A pre-alarm siren would then warn the more distant cities that they might be bombed since the German air defenses didn't yet know where the formations were headed. This time, Leipzig was the target, but the usual pre-alarm sirens to alert residents were silent. When the sirens finally signaled that a raid was imminent, bombs were already falling.

On the way to the shelter, Barbara "heard something crash in our living room." She told people in the cellar who went upstairs to our apartment and found a small bomb in flames on an armchair, which they threw out of a window. Our house had been hit, but the bombs were only small incendiaries that just penetrated into the top floors. In the cellar we saw flames flickering outside a small window; perhaps it was the burning armchair. Firefighters were busy elsewhere, so the fire slowly worked its way downstairs. We slept on bunk beds in the cellar of the next house. An old couple, Jehovah's Witnesses, died after they refused to go down to the cellar because they reportedly said that God willed them to die.

Much of the center of the city was on fire, which on a few streets mushroomed into fire storms. Our mother, who lived on the other side of town, had to run around the city center to reach us. She found us safe. I remember standing on the street the next morning, the air heavy and dark with smoke and paper flying about. By then, more than half the house had burned down. I recall seeing an Advent wreath swaying to and fro. Oma and Johanna, both in tears, pulled Barbara's doll carriage with some salvaged belongings. We walked to Johanna's rooftop apartment house, holding wet towels over our mouths and noses to filter out soot. The house was intact, but a window in our apartment was shattered.

I also vividly remember a large daytime raid by the US Air Force. American records list a daytime raid by 881 bombers on May 29, 1944, targeting industrial plants in the suburbs, some of which were close to where we lived. I had cut a toe and couldn't walk, so my mother carried me to the cellar, but not before we saw planes and their condensation trails. Once we were in the cellar, bombs began to whistle down, and as the whistling came closer, elderly women started to howl, a synchronized contrapuntal sound. We sat there with wet towels around our necks. A nasty old man, who later married Oma, sat beside a loose brick wall that opened to the next apartment house, but again our house was not hit.

Afterwards, I stood on a big pile of rubble watching an immense flame shooting out of the gym of a school, which apparently had been used by the military. There were lots of bomb craters, and Barbara and I collected antiaircraft shell fragments. Many more air raids took place in the fall of 1944 and did not cease until April 1945. I have no clear memories of them, but I do recall frequent stays in the cellar. In her 1947 letter to Alice Cook, our mother writes that "We weren't nearly as afraid of the ever-more severe air raids than of the Gestapo." I thought of the raid as a big adventure, not realizing then that Leipzig escaped the devastating air raids that hit Hamburg, Dresden, and Tokyo, in which huge firestorms killed tens of thousands. Schools closed in the fall of 1944.

US Liberation

American troops occupied Leipzig on April 18, 1945, three weeks before Germany's unconditional surrender and a week after my eighth birthday. There was shooting all day, because some German units fiercely resisted, while others simply discharged their weapons into the air. Fighting centered on the Monument of the Battle of the Peoples against Napoleon, a large fortified structure. Inhabitants hung white sheets from their windows to signal surrender.

In the morning, people went to loot some food stores, and sometime later the first American patrol moved cautiously down a wide street close to our house. We had spent most of the morning in the cellar, but in the absence of shooting in the vicinity, went upstairs to watch as a GI would run forward, crouch and aim, then run another ten steps followed by another. One GI, probably looking for snipers, took note of an apartment house across our side street which did not display white sheets.

Sherman tanks (I learned the name later) appeared, followed by rows of German POWs marching in the opposite direction with their arms up. Our mother cried. There were large numbers of US soldiers who had taken over various buildings. I asked one GI, who was standing guard outside a police station, "haf you chocolate?" and he responded with a rather cold, "No," probably because US soldiers were not then allowed to fraternize with Germans. Barbara was shocked to see that the GIs who stayed in a nearby requisitioned house had failed to turn out the lights at night.

One last atrocity was the murder by SS guards of inmates in a small concentration camp in a northern suburb of Leipzig who had been doing forced labor in industrial plants and were now trying to get away. After Leipzig capitulated, the Americans ordered people to see the bodies, including those which had been burned to death with flame throwers (Steinecke). The US military distributed leaflets and a newspaper for the German public. I read one, which was entitled, "Ihr sollt es wissen" (You must learn about it), that is, Nazi crimes; it contained photos of stacks of emaciated corpses. One detail that I remember was a description of inmates who were put into a cement mixer and crushed to death.

Johanna learned that thirty thousand liberated inmates in Theresienstadt were all very sick. Believing that Paul was among them, I recall seeing her kicking up her legs in despair. In her 1947 letter to Alice Cook, Johanna writes: "When the war ended we got the dreadful news about the concentration camps. Paul did not return and eventually I learned . . . that Paul had probably died on one of the transports or was murdered in Auschwitz." ("Transports" refers to the SS evacuation of the remaining inmates when Soviet troops were not far from the camp. En route, the SS killed thousands of them while others froze to death.) Johanna continues: "I collapsed. I don't know how I coped with this terrible news. I kept hoping in vain that he might still be alive."

Mentally and physically exhausted by the years of anxiety and stress, our mother had a nervous breakdown and was hospitalized for five months from late April to October. She also had a horrendous infection on her thigh that required a major operation. Barbara and I visited her and saw that her wound was wrapped in toilet paper. During these months, Gretel Weisske cared for us. She had a job with the railroads and brought us bean soup when there was very little to eat and also stood in long lines to buy food for us (*Dreams*, 65).

At first, I cried myself to sleep over my father's death, but then I adjusted. In occupied Germany, it was a source of honor, pride, and special privileges to have a relative who had died in a concentration camp. But over time, my father's murder had a lasting impact on me (see Chapter 8).

CHAPTER 6

Our Lives Since WWII: East Germany, 1945–1949

The First Three Years

In the fall of 1945, Johanna recovered and our situation substantially improved. In July 1945, the American military turned the provinces of Saxony and Thuringia over to the Soviets in exchange for the right to occupy West Berlin. I watched as a long column of Soviet soldiers marched into Leipzig with horse-drawn wagons. One of them shook my hand. The Soviet Military Administration in Germany, SMA, classified us as "Victims of Fascism" and allocated an apartment to us taken from an evicted Nazi family.

Our mother rejoined the SPD, but in 1946 the Soviet and German communists engineered the merger of the SPD with the KPD into the communist-dominated SED, which ruled the GDR until 1989. Johanna became editor of the culture page (*Feuilleton*) of the Leipzig *Volkszeitung* (People's Daily) and thus became a member of the local cultural elite.

Johanna began to publish poetry, novellas, and book reviews. She dedicated a collection of poems titled *Brennendes Leben* (Burning Life) to Paul's memory, the first poem of which is a very moving commemoration of his death. A play of hers, set in the kind of village in which we hid in the Sudetenland, is a dramatic story of a Nazi and an escaped concentration camp prisoner. I recall sitting in the front row and watching her receive a bouquet of flowers after the performance. She wore a shiny green dress, smiled, and looked beautiful.

Occasionally, during these hunger years, the local Soviet office in charge of cultural affairs would send a package containing raw meat. I remember that when Johanna went to meetings in Berlin, she would stuff food into her purse and bring it home. Barbara and I were sent several times to rest homes or farms, where more food was available than in Leipzig. During one such vacation, I learned how to herd cattle and milk cows. For my tenth birthday, our mother bought a bar of chocolate on the black market. Back home, there was no heat and little electricity. Aside from the food shortage, I recall collecting cigarette butts for my mother, who was then an avid smoker. I remember going to nearby fields to glean grain, and once I saw someone fainting in the street, probably from hunger.

In 1947, Johanna heard from Walter Raue—an old friend of Paul's—that Alice Cook had visited him in Berlin as a member of an American delegation sent to investigate the state of German trade unions and adult education. This news prompted our mother to write the letter quoted earlier, in which she describes our living conditions: "Paul's children give me endless joy. I can say that I live only for them, now 12 and 10. . . . When I now ask you for help, it is especially for them. They suffered during the Nazi years and there is now no way of meeting their needs." But Alice didn't receive this letter. On August 21,1947, our mother sent another one:

> Life here is becoming more and more difficult; we are afraid of the coming winter. To endure more hunger and cold seems impossible. . . . As I wrote in my last letter, is there some way to send the children abroad? Of course I would also like also to emigrate, but the British Consulate turned down our application because "people who were at war with Canada are not allowed to go there." What can I say about that? We suffered more than most—I lost the only person I ever loved aside from the children . . . yet we are now told that we are to blame for the war. I also don't think that I can expect favorable treatment from the US Consulate. The children are quite healthy but every day I have to struggle just to provide them with bread. Only God knows how long I can endure. And please write to me. It would be a great comfort to know that Paul has not been forgotten by his friends.

Alice did receive this letter, and after her return to the US started to send Care Packages to us, as well to her many German friends. The ones that we received were very welcome, of course.

Apart from the deprivations, these were good years for me as far as school and friends were concerned. At one point, my buddies and I threw stones at a hornets' nest, which turned out to have been a bad idea. I joined the Young Pioneers, the communist children's organization, a politicized version of the Boy Scouts. I took part in camping trips and learned to sing songs praising the wonders of the Soviet Union. Like all East German children, I started to learn Russian in the fifth grade. I remember our school taking note of the Chinese Communist Party's victory in October 1949. Barbara was also quite happy. She was terrific at writing stories, drawing pictures, and making things.

Johanna's Conflict with the Communist Authorities, 1948–1950

In about 1947, our mother left her newspaper job to edit *Maerz* (March), a new literary magazine, the title referring to the building of the new, socialist society. Her motive, she wrote, was to help raise the "horrifyingly low level of our cultural life" and to contribute to the building of a new, humane, socialist society. In a 1985 letter written to Jens Wehner, a German graduate student, who was working on a dissertation and wanted to know about her experiences with literary life in East Germany, she expressed her belief that socialism and freedom were compatible.

Maerz had been licensed by the Soviets on the strong recommendation of SED cadres. Johanna thought that they regarded her as a promising and talented rarity, someone who had stayed in Germany after 1933, was clearly an anti-fascist, and had not at all compromised with the Nazis. Some of these functionaries had suffered greatly in Nazi concentration camps, and so they supported her, even tolerating her mild deviations from the party line. Such cadres differed from those who returned from Soviet exile and who were much more dogmatic.

Initially, *Maerz* was a success. But in 1948, as the Cold War intensified, the Soviet Administration accused Johanna of misusing her position as editor- in- chief by accepting work with "cosmopolitan and West-oriented tendencies." "Cosmopolitan" referred to "rootless Jews," some of whom had taken to the streets in Moscow to celebrate the establishment of Israel, prompting the ever-paranoid Stalin to suspect a Zionist plot against him and to launch an antisemitic campaign that continued until his death in 1953.

Also in 1948, Stalin imposed a blockade on West Berlin which stopped supplies from reaching the city. In response, the US, Britain, and France organized a huge airlift to provide food and coal to the population. Stalin also ordered the Soviet satellites in Eastern Europe to give unconditional support to the Soviet Union in the struggle against the West, compelling their regimes to adopt without question the Soviet model of developing socialism. Until then, some communist leaders and officials had hoped to follow a more moderate "third way" between Stalin's socialism and Western capitalism. Officials charged with such deviations were ousted, imprisoned, or executed (Brzezinski, chapters 4–7).

In this harsh political environment, Johanna was in deep political trouble. Her license for *Maerz* had been granted on condition that she include writings by Soviet authors. Committed to upholding high literary standards, Johanna chose to publish high-quality Russian stories written long before the current era of Socialist Realism, a literary genre that required writers to depict contemporary life in a positive and affirming way. She did not publish contemporary Soviet work that she thought was formulaic and only echoed the party line. She felt repelled by writings that in effect crushed the freedom-oriented side of socialist ideology and downgraded good literature by promoting "petty-bourgeois, narrow and intolerant" work (letter to Jens Wehner). In addition to these offenses, she was accused of publishing Western work while ignoring East German writers who had returned from exile in the Soviet Union. Apparently, she knew that one of them, then a leading SED cultural official, had instigated the Soviet authorities to withdraw the license for *Maerz*.

Johanna was called to the Leipzig SED headquarters, attacked, berated, threatened, and ordered to undergo self-criticism. She responded innocently by saying that she couldn't understand what the fuss was all about. After all, she asked, don't we all share the same socialist ideals and the objective of publishing excellent writing? Some SED cadres felt that she should be given another chance to demonstrate her commitment to socialism and the working class by observing the lives of workers in an industrial enterprise near Leipzig. Alas, Johanna disappointed them by not portraying heroic workers enthusiastically building socialism, but instead wrote about their hard and difficult lives. In her words, this was an "unforgivable provocation" (letter to Jens Wehner).

As our mother's situation became increasingly precarious and, fearing arrest, she and her new husband, Gerhard Weidenmüller, fled to West Berlin, leaving their belongings behind and taking a circuitous route to avoid detection. Before leaving Leipzig in January 1950, she sent Barbara to her brother,

Uncle Willi, in Düsseldorf in the British zone, and me to Crailsheim in the American zone, to a couple who were enthusiastic readers of her work. In West Berlin Johanna and Gerhard were immediately recognized as political refugees.

Our mother had remarried in 1948, rightly believing that we needed a father. Gerhard had worked with Johanna at *Maerz*. She thought of him as a highly gifted individual, a promising writer, and an autodidact who was remarkably knowledgeable about literature, a quality that drew them together. They both disdained writing that didn't meet their high standards.

He was much younger than she and less mature. He was also emotionally very unstable. He publicly tore up his SED party card, adding to her political difficulties. Extremely jealous of Johanna's ongoing love for Paul and wanting her to forget him, he tore up many of Paul's photos and threw away his military decorations. Apparently, Johanna did not know about this, so we don't know whether or not she complained to him. In later years, I became very disturbed by Gerhard's effort to destroy my father's memorabilia.

At the time, however, I had positive feelings toward Gerhard. He became something of a father substitute. Furthermore, he was quite was amusing. Both he and Johanna liked to read highbrow fiction to us children. Our mother once asked whether we really understood the underlying meanings communicated by novelists such as Joseph Conrad. Neither of us, especially me, understood too much, and realizing that we were too young, Johanna and Gerhard stopped reading complex novels to us.

Gerhard very much wanted to adopt us, and Johanna asked us whether we agreed. Barbara told me later that she never did, but that our mother, badly in need of the domestic peace and quiet essential for her writing, pressed us to accept the idea and so we gave in. After our move to West Berlin, we enrolled in a boarding school, which permitted that even before the official adoption we could use Gerhard's name so that we wouldn't have to explain the name change to students at the school. In the end, and fortunately for us, the adoption did not materialize.

CHAPTER 7

Life in the West, 1950–the Present

West Germany, 1950–1953

I stayed in Crailsheim for about three months. My hosts were a businessman and his wife. I assisted him by doing minor clerical jobs for which he paid me. I stuck out because I spoke with a Saxonian dialect which was funny to people from other regions. When I left to travel to West Berlin and reunite with my mother, my hosts arranged for a truck to take me to the US-operated Frankfurt airport. As I walked to the gate to board the plane to Berlin for my first-ever plane trip, I noticed numerous "No Smoking" signs. In German, a "Smoking" is a tuxedo, so I was puzzled as to why people weren't allowed to wear tuxedos. Seeing the vast ruins of Berlin from above was quite a sight.

In West Berlin, Johanna and Gerhard set up a household and she resumed her writing career. Her first major novel, *Flight to Africa* (*Flucht nach Afrika*), appeared in 1952, won a prize, and was translated into English and other languages. Another, *Der Himmel Brennt* (The Sky is Burning,1955), is a fictionalized story about her experiences at the Leipzig industrial plant. Many more books followed, including *Dreams*.

Her literary activities did not provide an adequate income and Gerhard also was not able to make money. They received some social welfare benefits, but these were inadequate. They had difficulty paying for our education, but Alice Hanson Cook, who had returned to Germany to work for the Americans, greatly eased their financial burden by paying the tuition for a boarding school, the *Odenwaldschule* near Frankfurt, for Barbara and me.

This school was a progressive institution that sought to bridge the distance between teachers and students and resembled the Habertshof school of the 1920 (see Chapter 2). I adjusted well, but Barbara was asked to leave after a year or so because she didn't seem to fit in. An aggravating factor was an untreated thyroid deficiency that left her lethargic. But back in Berlin she was admitted to the Berlin Art Academy, even though she lacked a high school diploma, and successfully studied there until her emigration to America in 1960. I left the *Odenwaldschule* at the end of 1952 to prepare for emigration to the United States.

Alice's son Philip, was two years younger than I and also a student at the same boarding school. We became good friends. Alice was then going through a painful divorce, which seriously affected her son. She wrote in *A Lifetime of Labor* that "Phil went through a period of extreme distress" at the school and needed therapy" (131). Even without this crisis, adjusting to the German boarding school was hard for him. He was regarded as rather odd and he disliked the school's food. As for me, I especially hated the watery cottage cheese that we sometimes had to eat.

Alice once took Barbara and me to her Frankfurt apartment located in a US compound. Along the way she bought us milkshakes at an American snack bar, a tasty novelty. The American lifestyle and the things Americans seemed to take for granted were quite miraculous to us. In 1952, Phil and I went to the same summer camp in Switzerland, my first visit to a foreign country and my introduction to American teenage life.

In the summer of 1952, Alice and Philip returned to the US. Alice had been offered a job in the Extension Division of the School of Industrial and Labor Relations at Cornell University, where she was to teach members of trade union locals throughout New York State. Her early years at Cornell were marred by Senator Joseph McCarthy's notorious accusations of communist influence on American institutions, including trade unions. Guilt by association aroused suspicions about her, but she was not called to testify to the US Senate since the allegations against her lacked substance.

In 1955 Alice was appointed to a regular teaching position at Cornell's School of Industrial Relations, even though she didn't have a PhD. She had to learn how and what to teach undergraduate and graduate students, a big challenge because she had no prior professorial experience. Determined to succeed, she began to absorb as rapidly as possible the academic literature on trade unions in order to stay ahead of her students. "My sons (Philip and I) have told me that the summer of 1955 was one of constant reading" (148).

Her teaching, publications, and hard work eventually paid off and she was awarded tenure. Alice wrote about American and European trade unions and their educational programs and also spent a year in Japan doing research on the same general subject. She focused on women's double burden of balancing work with child care while getting less pay than their male counterparts. Her last big project was research on working women in nine countries. As a dedicated champion of women's liberation, she won renown at Cornell for her leadership in opening the men's Faculty Club to women. Toward the end of her career at the university, she was appointed Cornell's first ombudsman, which entailed a very challenging and difficult set of tasks, such as handling the grievances of Black students. She died in 1998.

Emigration to the US

In 1952, Alice invited me to live with her and Philip in the US, an offer that I greeted with great enthusiasm and wanted to accept. My mother agreed, but of course very reluctantly. In January 1953, I sailed to New York City, where Phil and his father, Wesley Cook, met me. We stayed in the city only long enough to visit the Empire State Building, which I badly wanted to see, before Phil and I went on to Ithaca. From then on, my mother and I maintained close contact via letters, phone calls, and, most important, periodic reunions in Berlin and in America.

My first trip to Europe, in the summer of 1956, was not to Germany, but to France and Britain because my mother feared that I might be drafted into the newly formed West German army. While I had a US Green Card for permanent residence, I was still a German citizen. When I turned eighteen, I registered for the US Selective Service System, but was never drafted because of educational deferments, and also because I became a father in 1968. When we met, my mother, Barbara, and I travelled around Britain and stayed in Paris for a few weeks. After my naturalization in 1958, I regularly visited her in Germany and she also visited us in America.

My life with Alice and Philip was an extraordinary change for me. Alice became my second mother and Philip a brother. In the summer of 1953, he and I biked from Ithaca to Traverse City, Michigan, where his grandfather owned a cherry orchard. We got paid for picking cherries and met migrant farm workers. After our return, I worked at various part-time jobs to reduce the financial burden on Alice, since her salary at Cornell was then quite small. In the summers of 1954 and 1955 I had a job assisting a graduate student at Cornell's School of Agriculture with his research on growing vegetables in different types of soil, requiring visits to appropriate sites in New York State.

Alice worked hard to be a good mother to two rambunctious teenagers. Once, she took us to Ithaca's Butterfield Park in midwinter, where we walked on an ice-covered path, which later was closed as too dangerous. Alice climbed with heroic persistence over large ice clumps as a waterfall roared just a few feet away. Being a mother clearly had its slippery side! When I was learning to drive, Alice was once in the car with me when I lost control going down a steep hill, and although we didn't crash, she sensibly stopped riding with me. At one point, she took me to a nearby Native American reservation, but wrote that I was "bitterly disappointed" since I didn't find the heroic warriors that I had read about in Germany (Cook, 138).

Alice played a major role in easing my adaptation to American life. She and Phil were fluent German-speakers, but we switched to English after only a few months. Alice also taught me how to write proper English. My mother later complained that while my letters to her were in German, they were heavily anglicized. I learned a lot from Alice about US culture, the labor movement, and the many progressive causes that she supported. When Eli Kazan's film *On the Waterfront* was shown in Ithaca, Alice was all set to protest against what she thought was a union-busting film. I suggested that she ought first to see it and she then agreed that it was not.

When I started school, Alice consulted with Ithaca High School about where to place me. My English was still deficient and I had not been exposed to subjects such as social studies. I entered as a freshman, Alice wrote, as a way of "giving him the least stress" (Cook, 137). The school told me to take a vocational class and the one that I chose was to learn to set type. Later, I was taught how to use a use a typewriter, an essential skill. Most of my courses were on the academic side. Alice recalled that a teacher of German took me under her wing as a helpful native speaker. I was involved in some school activities, made a few friends, and went out on some dates. I liked the school, but was struck by the ignorance of some students, one of whom asked me whether Germany had electricity. I graduated in 1955 and started college at Harvard.

In those years, I came to love Alice. I admired her many accomplishments, her skill at networking and maintaining long-term friendships, her political beliefs, her courage, integrity, and determination to succeed and cope with adversity. She inspired me to overcome the negative outlook on life that I had grown up with. She was my role model, but I can't claim that I was all that successful in emulating her.

In the summer of 1953, our substitute father, Gerhard, also emigrated to Ithaca with the idea of paving the way for Johanna and Barbara to join us once he had earned sufficient money. He found jobs delivering messages, worked on construction projects, and was hired by the Ithaca telephone company, which offered to train him. But, as Alice recalled, "it became clear that he had neither the desire nor the intention to bring Johanna and Barbara to America," because he wanted to excel as a writer, a goal that for him took precedence over everything else. Alas, he failed in this endeavor. He became mentally ill and the "Ithaca police sent him to nearby Willard State Psychiatric hospital" (146–147). After his release, he was deported to Germany. Although Johanna had divorced him, he appealed to her to pay for his return to Germany. Feeling sorry for him, Johanna did so and allowed him to live in her apartment. Unfortunately, his paranoia caused her endless trouble with the neighbors. He died suddenly in 1988—his was a sad, failed life.

After I started college, I kept in touch with Philip, meeting him every so often. He studied at Cornell and engaged in political activities, but was expelled after an arrest on a drug charge. Alice was of course deeply upset about this new crisis in his life. Ellen Bernstein (my then wife) and I tried to be supportive. He escaped having to go to jail, apparently because he volunteered to enlist in the army, and was stationed first in Korea and then in Germany. After his stint in the military, he worked in a steel mill in Buffalo, NY, and joined its trade union, but had to quit because of a serious work injury.

From then on, Phil's life took off. He returned to college, this time the University of Buffalo, and earned a PhD with a thesis on ethnic politics in that city. He used his connections with the local Democratic Party to get an appointment as treasurer for the city of Buffalo. He went on to serve as director of the Office of Management and Budget of the New York State Legislature, and continued to be active politically in the Democratic Party. Later, he was appointed executive director of the Erie County Water Authority and also ran a polling business with his second wife, Hope Cook. In 1985, he suffered a heart attack, but recovered. Ellen and I visited him in an Albany Hospital. Ten years later, he lost his Erie County directorship due to a conflict with a local politician. His last job was as a consultant on water management in China. There, he had a second heart attack and died in early 2001. I spoke at his memorial service in Buffalo.

Our Mother's Battle to Obtain Restitution

After its establishment in 1949, the West German government set up the Entschädigungsamt (Restitution Office), a state agency to handle compensation for victims of Nazi persecution. Our mother applied for these funds, but had to wage a tenacious struggle mainly from 1951 to 1959, and again in 1965 and in 1994–1995 to get her claims approved. Her large restitution file makes for painful reading (Landesarchiv-Berlin). The main issue was inadequate documentation. Again and again, she had to explain to skeptical and suspicious officials and courts why it was so difficult to obtain substantiating evidence for her claims. Oaths were not sufficient. The process was arduous and emotionally and physically draining.

Some of her claims were eventually approved, but others were denied, leading to appeals, reapplications, and law suits. Johanna petitioned top-level officials, including the mayor of West Berlin and the chancellor of the federal government, and these efforts may have helped in getting the Restitution Office to take her claims seriously.

Johanna sought to obtain a widow's pension for herself, funds for the education of her children, plus compensation for confiscated property and the loss of work opportunities during the twelve years of the Nazi regime. Even the seemingly straightforward request for educational support was at first denied because our mother was still alive and we were not full orphans. Johanna pointed out that war orphans who also had living mothers were readily given stipends and asked the office why it turned down the victims of Nazi terror. After four years of correspondence, the authorities finally relented and Barbara and I received education stipends. I was able to leave my part-time jobs at Harvard and, later, at Columbia.

Johanna's lost work opportunities also raised major questions because she was a freelance writer. She reported that the volume of poetry that could not be published in 1933 because of her Jewish husband was evidence of her productivity. She argued that had she been able to publish in the 1930s, she would have gained the reputation and name recognition essential for reaching an audience. She argued that this explained why her postwar book sales were meager. Her claim for compensation for her inability to advance in her profession from 1933 on was denied.

Johanna was also asked to provide evidence about her nonliterary jobs and contributions to the German employee's pension fund. She told the

Restitution Office the story of her quest for work from 1939 to 1944. Some documentation was found, but witnesses were either dead or could not be reached in East Germany. She was able to submit evidence of her jobs after the war as an employee of a Leipzig newspaper and as editor of the journal *Maerz,* and also to prove that in 1948 she was forbidden to publish because of her conflict with the communist regime. In West Berlin, she received unemployment benefits based on her Leipzig work record, but only for several years. Except for a temporary job at an American library, she had to subsist on her rather meager book royalties until her pension was granted in 1956.

The size of her widow's pension hinged on Paul's earnings, which in 1932 were substantial but then ceased entirely. Because of the 1939 divorce, she had to submit long explanations to a court that she was forced to divorce by the Nazi regime, but that their relationship continued afterwards and that Paul had sent child support payments until his deportation. The Restitution Office determined the civil service rank that he would have achieved without the persecution. Johanna complained that the rank was far below the one it should have been, but to no avail.

Similarly, Johanna's property claims were difficult to substantiate. She asked to be reimbursed for the furniture which she and Paul had donated in 1932 to the youth home for young unemployed workers (see Chapter 2). The Nazis had stolen it, but Johanna and Paul had no records regarding the furniture. She also wanted to be compensated for the huge book collection that she and her husband had inherited. Some of the volumes were very valuable first editions, and a number of them had been published as early as the seventeenth century.

Her request to be compensated for the very expensive jewelry that our parents had inherited was denied. One item was a heavy goblet made of gold on which the names of generations of the Bernstein family were inscribed. As noted above, selling the jewels had been the major source of their income from 1933 on. Paul had receipts for both the sales and for the jewelry confiscated by the Gestapo, but they were lost when he was deported.

In 1956, Johanna obtained a pension from the Restitution Office freeing her from having to rely on honoraria alone. In addition, the three of us received lump sum payments called *Kapitalentschädigung* (capital restitution), apparently compensation for property and job losses. Johanna believed that these funds were far less than the value of the family's actual losses.

University, Career, Marriage

At Harvard College, I majored in government, following my father's footsteps. I specialized in Soviet affairs, building on the Russian language that I had started to learn in East Germany. After I graduated cum laude in 1959, I entered Columbia University for graduate study in political science with a Russian specialization. Two years later, I added a second subfield, communist China, after taking an exciting course about that country. My goal was to compare how the Soviet Union and China went about building socialism. With a Foreign Area Fellowship, I was able to do this.

Chinese, however, was much more difficult to learn than Russian. My first Chinese teacher once told the class that I was "the inventor of toneless Chinese." I learned to read Chinese sources for my dissertation and later research projects, and managed to become somewhat fluent and able to interview refugees in Hong Kong and in China when research there became possible. I also did some research in the Soviet Union. In my doctoral thesis, I sought to explain why the collectivization of agriculture in Russia was extremely coercive, causing enormous suffering among the peasants, but the process was less harsh in the People's Republic of China. In 1970, I received a PhD "with Distinction." Two of my research articles analyzed the man-made famines in China and the Soviet Union that in both countries caused millions of deaths.

My first teaching job was in 1966–69 at Indiana University, followed by six years at Yale, and then thirty-two years at Columbia from 1975 to my retirement in 2007. I served as department chair for two terms and I enjoyed teaching and doing research. By 2013, I had sponsored or co-sponsored seventy-two dissertations. I wrote nearly fifty academic articles and book chapters, some co-authored, and many book reviews and review articles. Publishing books, however, was very difficult, as I explain in Chapter 8.

In 1961, I married Ellen Hauser. Her parents, as well as Alice, Philip, Barbara, and friends came to the wedding. Unfortunately, my mother was not able to take part. Ellen had just graduated from Smith College with a major in history, and worked as an editor and a teacher of the Lamaze birthing method. She and I spent 1964 in Hong Kong, where she taught history at a secondary girls' school while I was doing doctoral research. We returned to the US via India, Afghanistan, the Soviet Union, and Poland, where we visited Auschwitz before going to Berlin. Ellen and I were devoted parents, and raising our two daughters, Anya and Maia, brought us much joy. However, in 1990 Ellen and I divorced and soon thereafter I married Dorothy Solinger.

Maia graduated from the Columbia School of General Studies with a major in English. She began her career in academic administration at Columbia and is now at Barnard College, where she is currently the administrator for three academic programs. The college greatly values her dedication and hard work. Maia has strong interests in philosophy, poetry, and psychology, reads widely, writes beautifully, and enjoys singing with me.

Anya graduated from Barnard College and earned a PhD from the Department of Government at Harvard. Her dissertation, published in 2021, was titled "The Moderation Dilemma: Legislative Coalitions and the Politics of Family and Medical Leave." She spent twenty-five years teaching at Harvard and serving as Director of Undergraduate Studies for the Committee on Degrees in Social Studies, an interdisciplinary undergraduate program. In 2023, she moved to Brown University to become the faculty director of the International and Public Affairs Concentration (a major) at the Watson Institute. Tragically, Anya died suddenly in August 2024.

In 1994, Anya married Jonathan Bassett in a sparkling ceremony. Jon graduated from Columbia College and Brown University and is a highly talented high school history teacher. In 2021, he and a colleague published *From Story to Judgment: The Four Question Method for Teaching Social Studies*. The four methods are: 1. Narration: What happened?; 2. Interpretation: What were they thinking?; 3. Explanation: Why then and there?; 4. Judgment: What do we think about this? The authors have been visiting school districts around the country to talk about their approach. I wish that I had known about these ideas when I started to teach.

Anya and Jon's son, Benjamin Paul, graduated from Kenyon College, majoring in politics. He was inspired to learn German after our family trip to Berlin in 2015 and returned to Berlin to study abroad. I have practiced German with him and we engage in spirited political discussions. He is a political consultant who works on the transition to green energy.

Their daughter, Sarah, graduated in 2023 from the University of Vermont, specializing in early childhood education. She received major awards for her work at UVM and teaches first grade in Burlington, Vermont. She is also a dedicated dancer.

My second wedding, to Dorothy J. Solinger (Dorie), was a Jewish ceremony and a new experience for me. Dorie introduced me to the Jewish faith and its customs. We started going together to High Holiday services and observe Passover. Eventually, we joined a Reconstructionist synagogue in Irvine, California. I did not formally convert to Judaism, but enjoy the services, rituals, the singing, and the programs.

Dorie was born in Cincinnati in 1945. My two daughters, Alice, Barbara, Philip, and his second wife, Hope, came to our wedding, as did Dorie's mother and others in her family, as well as Columbia colleagues and friends. Alice wrote that after Philip's and my divorces "I readily established an enjoyable, collegial, as well as a familial, relationship with their second wives" (194).

Dorie graduated from the University of Chicago, and earned a PhD at Stanford in comparative politics with a China subfield, which brought us together. We first met when she visited Yale in 1969 to learn about its China program and attended a lecture of mine on Chinese politics. In the years that followed, we met at scholarly meetings and conferences in the US and abroad, made many research trips to China, and fell in love. In 2004, we went to a China conference in Poland and visited Auschwitz, the second time for me. I learned a lot from Dorie about social life, maintaining friendships, and staying connected to others. I came to share her deep love for classical music, theater, opera, and world travel. Like Ellen, who edited my dissertation, Dorie has edited many of my writings. We are a very happily married couple.

Dorie had a distinguished career teaching and doing research, first at the University of Pittsburgh (1975–1984) and then at the University of California, Irvine (1986–2016). She has published far more books than I on topics such as rural migration to Chinese cities and urban poverty. Dorie's spoken Chinese is also much better than mine because she succeeded in mastering Chinese tones, which I have always found difficult.

Until my retirement from Columbia in 2007, our marriage was bicoastal. We lived together for about eight months of each year, as Dorie took leaves of absence from UCI to do research and writing at Columbia and I spent summers and sabbaticals in Irvine. Dorie and I stayed in regular contact with Alice Cook, including visits on her birthdays, and family reunions at Thanksgiving together with Philip and Hope. As her health deteriorated, Alice talked with both Philip and me about her planned move to an assisted living community. I spoke at her memorial service.

From the late 1980s on, our mother's health got worse. She had long lived with heart trouble, but now her eyesight worsened, affecting her mobility and capacity to read and write. A good friend, Ruth Ellerbrock, provided much needed help to enable Johanna to continue writing, and also brought meals. Barbara and I visited Johanna at least once a year and sought to arrange additional help and medical care. She naturally wanted us to come and live with her in Berlin, but our jobs in the US made that impossible.

During my visits, I rented cars and drove her around West Berlin. After the collapse of communist rule and Germany's reunification in 1990, I was able to take her to the Bernstein grave in East Berlin. I had arranged for grave plaques to be placed for Paul, his brother, Richard, and his aunt Regina, greatly moving our mother.

In the late 1990s, Johanna became seriously ill with pancreatic cancer and was hospitalized. Both Barbara and I visited her every day in her hospital. She passed away on June 21, 2000, at the age of eighty-nine. Dorie, Barbara, and I were present at her funeral.

CHAPTER 8

Legacies of the Nazi Past

After the war, Johanna, Barbara, and I sought to come to grips with the tragedies that befell our family. Johanna never got over Paul's murder and expressed her grief in her books and poems. She was deeply ambivalent about her native country. She stayed there for cultural and literary reasons, but was always very critical of German society. She was especially incensed by the long failure of Germany to face up to the Nazi past. One notorious example is that of Hans Globke, who for ten years from 1953 to 1963 was secretary of state and chief of staff in Chancellor Konrad Adenauer's government. As a high official in the Office of Jewish Affairs of the Ministry of the Interior during the Nazi regime, he co-authored the official legal commentary on the Nuremberg race laws. Another of his anti-Jewish measures was the directive that forced Jews to accept Israel and Sara as their middle names (Wikipedia, "Globke").

After the war, Johanna severed her relations with the Catholic Church because of its continued adherence to patriarchal principles and because of the complicity of Pope Pius XII with the Nazi regime. (Recent research, however, reveals a more complex picture of his behavior; see Gallagher and Parks). Still, before her death she asked that Barbara and I arrange a Catholic funeral, which we did. A priest, Hubert Schöning, presided. His eulogy quoted from her poetry and eloquently evoked what he thought the past must have meant to her. Speaking of "the dark years of the brown madness," he said:

> a fever of contempt for the world and for mankind poisoned a people of culture. The horror of these events entered her life and inflicted deep and irreparable harm. It destroyed her love, plunged her husband into the abyss, and forced her to flee in order to save her children. There are few rhymes in her

> poems, no periods or commas; perhaps I may interpret this as a consequence of the violation of the human order, of ethics, and the perversion of the powers-that-be. . . .
>
> What has Germany not done to her? We can only suspect. Yet, she found strength to keep going in dignity, her head up, and impassioned for justice (Schöning in Venske, 2001, 177–183).

Barbara has always mourned our father's death, especially since she has more direct memories of him than me. She shares her mother's feelings about Germany. Her experiences during the Nazi years led her to distrust strangers, whom she has often kept at bay. She has always been suspicious of the motives of others. In the US, she has continued to paint and mostly lived alone in Ithaca with two cats while earning a living doing biological drawings at Cornell.

As for me, my father's death made my university career more difficult and less successful than it might have been. I think the cause may have been survivor's guilt over my father's fate. He was unable to reach his fullest potential because his career was abruptly cut off in 1933, so how could I fulfill mine? Such feelings affected my writing of books. At the universities where I taught, publishing books was the way to achieve status and prestige, and I lagged sharply behind many of my colleagues. With each major writing project, I fell into serious depressions, making completion much more prolonged and painful, sometimes leading to the abandonment of a work in progress. Despite much effort, I did not succeed in revising my thesis for publication. I am grateful to both Ellen and Dorie, who have been highly supportive during my bouts with depression. Since I actually achieved quite a lot in my academic career, I can't claim that my life has been dominated by the legacy of my father's fate. I have written one book, co-authored another, and co-edited a third, all well received.

The Nazi era affected my identity as half-German and half-Jewish. Rather than anglicizing my surname when I became a US citizen, I added Paul as a middle name to signify my heritage. Fellow students, professors, and others assumed that I was Jewish. I was familiar with the history of American antisemitism and occasionally I encountered a few unpleasant examples. The overall situation was radically different. As Franklin Foer wrote in "The Golden Age of American Jews Is Ending," American Jewry benefited from the spread of liberalism in society and politics which led to an

> unprecedented period of safety, prosperity, and political influence. Jews, who had once been excluded from the American establishment, became full-fledged members of it. And remarkably, they achieved power by and large without having to abandon their identity . . . they infused the wider culture with that identity. . . . Their anxieties became American anxieties. Their dreams became American dreams.
>
> But that era is drawing to a close.

I am indeed as ambivalent about Germany as my mother and sister. I certainly don't share my father's unconditional love for his "fatherland." In the US I have rarely talked about my German background, preferring people to ask. I was pleased when on a visit to Germany someone remarked that for a foreigner my German was pretty good. Because of resentments over Nazi crimes, I have tried to avoid being identified with Germany. In my first year at Harvard, we were shown *Triumph of the Will,* Leni Riefenstahl's film about the 1934 Nazi Party rally in Nuremberg, followed by a shocking film about the liberation of Nazi concentration camps. To my chagrin, a roommate remarked that it was "your countrymen" who committed such terrible crimes. Despite my familiarity with the country, I did not specialize in German studies and instead chose to work on China and Russia. I did not encourage my daughters to learn German, but my grandson did and spent a semester studying in Berlin.

As this book demonstrates, some Germans took great risks by helping our family, exemplified by Prelate Lichtenberg, who prayed for the persecuted Jews and died en route to Dachau, and the managers of the Leipzig firm who hired Johanna despite Nazi grumbling (see Henry's article and Monroe's book on the subject). A good many German communists, social democrats, liberals, conservatives, and army officers engaged in resistance activities—such as Hans von Dohnanyi and his relative, Dietrich Bonhoeffer, a well-known theologian and a relentless and courageous opponent of the Nazis. He alerted ecumenical groups abroad about the great threat Hitler represented. He joined a dissident group of Protestant pastors, the Confessing Church, and more than eight hundred of its members were arrested and jailed in 1937. After the 1944 failure of the last attempt to assassinate Hitler, "As many as 6,000 people were rounded up, tried, and most of them executed," including Dohnanyi and Bonhoeffer (Sifton and Stern). Moltke was also put to death.

I wrote my senior thesis on German resistance to Hitler to understand how much had actually occurred, since fellow students and professors were quite skeptical. I found out much later that some anti-Nazi conservatives retained their traditional antisemitic sentiments despite their opposition to the regime. One of them, the former mayor of Leipzig, Carl Goerdeler, wrote a manifesto calling for the creation of a haven abroad for Jewish survivors, but would allow only Jewish veterans to regain their German citizenship. He was executed in 1944 (Geheran, 144; Dipper).

I admire enormously the great efforts that Germany has made to atone for and commemorate the Holocaust, a part of what was called *Vergangenheitsbewältigung* (coming to terms with the past). Despite public indifference, in 1953 the West German government started to pay large-scale reparations to Israel and extend compensation to survivors of the Holocaust. In the 1960s, the German public became much more aware of Nazi crimes due to the trial of Adolf Eichmann in Israel and numerous court cases brought against Nazi criminals by German prosecutors, such as the trial of Auschwitz officers. The Holocaust also became part of the required school curriculum.

Some years ago, a German movement got underway to commemorate Jewish victims by placing *Stolpersteine* (stumbling stones) on streets where these people had lived as a reminder of their fates. The stones list the name, date of birth, and year of deportation and murder. In 2012, Dorie and I, accompanied by Regula Venske, Johanna's close literary friend, witnessed the installation of a *Stolperstein* for our father. There also are such memorials for Paul's older brother, Richard, and for cousin Toni Witkowski, but I am not sure about others in the family. I contributed my father's story to a popular permanent exhibition about 158 Jews who had lived near his Berlin home, entitled *Wir Waren Nachbarn—Biographien jüdischer Zeitzeugen* (We Were Neighbors—Biographies of Jewish Witnesses). All this, together with the fact that Germany became a stable democracy, greatly attenuated my negative feelings. Germany's contemporary right-wing radicalism has, however, tempered any growing sympathies.

An extraordinary incident occurred in 1970. It concerned Willy Brandt, the leader of the SPD who returned to Germany from exile in 1945 and served as mayor of West Berlin from 1957 to 1966 and chancellor of West Germany from 1969 to 1974. On a visit to Poland, he fell to his knees at the Warsaw Memorial of the 1943 Ghetto Uprising. His *Kniefall* was widely applauded abroad and at home. Yet almost 50 percent of West Germans thought his gesture was "excessive" (Wikipedia, "Willy Brandt"). German remorse is symbolized by the huge Monument to the Murdered Jews of Europe, which is located at the center of Berlin, close to the Brandenburg Gate.

At the same time, resurgent far-right forces oppose Holocaust commemorations. These are not only neo-Nazis, but also include the populist, far-right party Alternative for Germany (Alternative für Deutschland, AfD). In early 2017, Björn Höcke, at the time the head of the branch of the AfD in the state of Thuringia province branch of the party, spoke to a gathering of members of the AfD's youth organization (Young Alternative for Germany) and demanded that Germany turn fully away from the "country's culture of remembrance." He asked whether the Berlin monument that commemorates the Holocaust was a "Denkmal der Schande" (Monument of Shame). This prompted a critical response. Some Germans asked whether he meant that the monument itself was shameful or whether he thought of it as a memorial to a shameful past. He later claimed that he only meant the latter, but then he also condemned the

> "idiotic policy of overcoming the legacy of the past [*dämliche Bewältigungspolitik*] which today is still paralyzing us. We don't need rites for the dead. We Germans are the only people in the world that built a monument of shame in the heart of the capital" (Quoted in Kammen).

The young AfD members greeted his speech with hearty applause.

Watching American soldiers free us from Hitler's grasp also had a long-term positive impact on me. After I came to the US, I found it difficult to criticize this country publicly. Other Holocaust survivors in America shared this mindset because of our deep gratitude to the country. At the same time, I was well aware of the history of slavery and the racial discrimination that persists to this day. I recall debating with Harvard classmates from the South who objected to the historic Supreme Court desegregation decision of 1954. And I have avidly followed political developments in the US, voted regularly, contributed money to candidates, and on occasion written letters to newspapers on current issues.

Another reason for not emulating my father's intense political activism was anxiety lest it arouse suspicions about my real allegiance. I learned from Alice Cook how easily demagogues such as Senator McCarthy can accuse people of having had communist associations. I thought that my specialization on communist regimes might cause problems, in part because in the 1960s, the post office notified me that I was receiving Chinese communist propaganda. Also, I didn't participate in the anti-Vietnam war movement, worrying that it might lead to the revocation of my citizenship. These anxieties proved groundless.

EPILOGUE

Contrasting German and American Approaches to Today's Far-Right Extremists (April 2024)

Germany's Reaction to the Nazi Past

In recent years, both countries have been challenged by an upsurge of radical right-wing movements. In both, democracy is under threat and the outcome of far-right activities is uncertain. But the danger for democracy is immeasurably greater in America than in Germany.

One reason for the difference is that Germany reacted sharply to the Nazi catastrophe. In line with the philosopher George Santayana's injunction that "those who do not remember the past are condemned to repeat it," the designers of postwar Germany's economic and political system sought to create institutions able to resist the rise of another dictatorship.

In the economic realm, the leaders of the Federal Republic of Germany understood that the gross economic and political inequalities characteristic of the Weimar period had fueled resentments that Hitler exploited in his ascent to power. As a remedy, they chose to establish a "social market economy." Thomas F. Remington analyzes its meaning in his pathbreaking study *Returns to Power: A Political Theory of Economic Inequality,* which includes a telling comparison with the United States. He writes that the West Germans

> believed that economic freedom and economic growth must serve basic values of freedom, equality, and justice. They argued that market freedom must be protected by government, but government must also ensure that all sections of

> society benefit from its fruits. Competition must underpin freedom for individuals in both the political and economic arenas; government must work to prevent the accumulation of private power that would threaten freedom. . . . These principles have remained foundational to this day (259–260).

The results are that "Vigorous party competition has tended to produce a pull towards compromise and centrism in German politics" (287):

> In the political arena, it is notable that no ruling group has mounted an assault on the political rights of its opponents. German liberalization never permitted business or government to sabotage workers' rights as it did in the United States (258).

The process of balancing the interests of labor with those of business via collective bargaining generated political controversies and necessitated incremental political adjustments as international and domestic conditions changed. The absorption of the GDR into the Federal Republic of Germany in 1990 caused immense stress. Resentment over how it was imposed contributed to much stronger support for right-wing parties. Still, Remington concludes that "Germany's postwar history warrants a cautiously optimistic view of Germany's ability to surmount these problems" (280).

The contrast with American economic and political developments since the 1970s is stark:

> the cumulative effect of the alliance of corporate economic power with conservative political forces . . . has moved American policy ever further to the right, to the point of subverting fair electoral competition entirely. . . . [T]he concentrated power of the Right has used its influence in electoral, regulatory, and judicial institutions to erode the redistributive potential of majority rule (287).

An example is the 2010 Citizens United vs. Federal Election Commission"(FEC) case, in which the conservative majority of the Supreme Court decided that the right of free speech guaranteed under the First Amendment also applies to corporations and rich donors. As a consequence of this ruling, they can now spend unlimited amounts of money to boost right-wing candidates during election campaigns and support conservative causes. This has tilted the playing field sharply to the Right. (Ibid, 315) "No clearer emblem of its threat to democracy is the presidency of Donald Trump".

A second major lesson from the Nazi period is found in the 1949 constitution, the *Grundgesetz* (Basic Law), that incorporates clauses designed to block the rise of another dictator. Its framers knew well that Hitler's ascent to power had actually been facilitated by the Weimar Constitution (1919). The contrast with the United States is striking.

First, the Basic Law omitted Article 48, which gave the president of the republic major powers to act unilaterally. He was directly elected by the people, and was empowered to rule by decree in cases of dire emergency, such as the devastating Great Depression of the early 1930s. In those years, the legislature, the Reichstag, was bitterly divided and unable to agree on measures needed to cope with this crisis. President Hindenburg's rule by decree began in 1930 and culminated in 1933, when he appointed Adolf Hitler Chancellor (see Chapter 2).

In contrast, the Basic Law stipulates that the president cannot legislate by decree in cases of great emergency, and also that he is not chosen by the electorate at large but by the majority of members of the Federal Assembly, the Bundestag, and by representatives elected by the legislatures of Germany's states. These changes turned the presidency into a largely ceremonial post, similar to the heads of state in many parliamentary democracies. Presidents can, of course, still use their prestige and moral authority to influence public opinion.

Second, the Basic Law stipulates that a parliamentary vote of no confidence in the chancellor cannot become effective before the Bundestag has chosen a successor. This clause avoids an interregnum which could stymie the holdover government, a gap that deepened the Weimar Republic's instability.

Third, the postwar framers changed Weimar's reliance on proportional representation, which enabled small parties to promote various parochial causes. In the 1930 elections, for instance, five major parties competed, but so did thirty-two minor ones. The Basic Law stipulates that a party cannot be represented in the Bundestag unless it has the support of 5% or more of the electorate. None of the small parties of 1930 met this threshold. As of 1927, the Nazi Party had the support of only 2.6% of the electorate, before it leapt forward during the Depression, when it gained 18.25% of votes in 1930 (Wikipedia, "German Federal Election data").

Fourth, and most important, the framers of the Basic Law sought to create a "militant, defensive democracy," following the

> idea that government authority and the law can be used to *exclude* and *aggressively* prosecute anti-democratic forces. . . . [The framers] wrote a constitution that allowed for the *banning* and *restricting* of insurrectionist or "anti-constitutional" speech, groups, and parties. . . . Used on rare occasions to investigate extremist left-and right-wing parties . . . the mere existence of this authority to investigate groups that assault "the democratic order" arguably has a deterrent effect on extremist forces. The model has spread over much of Europe (Levitsky and Ziblatt, *Tyranny*, 2023, 227–228, *authors' italics*).

To enforce these provisions, the Federal Office for the Protection of the Constitution (Bundesamt für Verfassungschutz, BfV) was set up, which is empowered to investigate the "rise of political forces that could once again usurp the democracy from the inside." Such measures require judicial approval (Poll). Altogether, since its inception, the BfV has banned twenty left- and right-wing extremist groups and parties, including many neo-Nazis (Kavi and Schuetze).

However, these safeguards have not prevented the rise of far-right forces because formidable legal and political obstacles stand in the way of their implementation. A case in point is the Alternative für Deutschland (AfD), mentioned above for its opposition to the commemoration of the Holocaust. It is populist and nationalist, signified by the slogan, "Unser Land Zuerst" (Our Country First). It was established in 2013 to oppose the mainstream parties that have governed the country since 1949 because, the AfD claims, they have failed to stand up for Germany. The party calls for preserving state sovereignty and agitates for maintaining German identity, culture, and language, and for abandoning multiculturalism. It also demands the restoration of the Weimar provision for the popular election of the president and the use of plebiscites to empower the people (AfD, "Grundsatzprogram für Deutschland"). It also opposes the European Union. As one of its leaders declared, "this EU must die for the true Europe to live" (Fix and Stelzenmüller).

At the center of its program is opposition to large-scale immigration. The party bitterly criticizes the government's willingness to take in huge numbers of foreigners, as it did when Chancellor Angela Merkel admitted a million refugees in 2015, assuring the public that "wir schaffen dass" (we can handle this). The party's adherents see unchecked immigration as a threat to public safety, which calls for a stronger police force and harsher laws. As a consequence, it has attracted more members of the police and the armed forces. The AfD is hostile to Muslims who wish to preserve their way of life, especially in organized form. German business elites, however, have criticized the AfD, since Germany needs many skilled foreign workers (*Economist*).

The AfD rejects all measures aimed at mitigating global warming. It argues that transitioning away from reliance on fossil fuels is too expensive. To the contrary, it calls for the restoration of Russia's gas pipeline (Nord Stream) and for the reactivation of nuclear power plants (Budras).

Russia's invasion of Ukraine also increased support for the party because the sanctions imposed on Russia and the cost of aid to Ukraine exacerbated inflation. The AfD and other right-wing groups want to improve relations with Russia and sympathize with Putin's strongman rule.

Support for the AfD is particularly robust in the eastern states, the former GDR (German Democratic Republic), where unification has not brought the hoped-for economic benefits. Intense anti-immigrant sentiments are widespread and there is more discrimination, as well as violence, directed at migrants than in former West Germany. Support is particularly high in poorer districts, where people feel resentful and left behind. These people long for a lost past and believe that their best days are behind them. They see a future with little hope, believe the country is in decline, and feel that Germany has changed too rapidly for them to keep up (Richter).

In January 2024, opinion polls in the eastern states showed that "well above 30 percent" of respondents favor the AfD (Schuetze, January 21, 2024). In Saxony and Thuringia, the AfD succeeded in electing enough deputies to the provincial legislatures to make them eligible to take positions in coalition governments.

An interviewee in Thuringia told reporters that "'whoever votes for the AfD must know that they have the Nazis in tow.'" This elicited "'hate mail and threatening phone calls. . . . People are afraid to take a stand against the AfD and that makes us more worried than anything else" (Grieshaber). And in Bavaria, in 2023, the AfD and another right-wing party won a combined total of 30.4% in a state election (Fix and Stelzenmüller). Stephen Kramer, the head of the state's Office for the Protection of the Constitution (BfV), who is Jewish, commented that if the AfD enters the state government "'he and his family will leave the country. . . . We've seen before in history where that can lead'" (Grieshaber).

Members of the party vary in their views; some are relatively moderate. But with the increase in the party's popularity, an "insurgent internal wing" has succeeded in pushing the party in an even more radical direction. Attacks on immigrants by AfD members and neo-Nazis rose by 73% from 2021 to 2022.

In 2017, in the Federal Republic of Germany as a whole, 13% of the electorate voted for the AfD, greatly in excess of the 5% threshold. It became the largest opposition party and the first far-right party since 1949 to enter the Bundestag. In 2021, its support dropped to 10%, but according to a January 2024 opinion poll, increased to nearly 25% in 2024 (Schuetze, January 21, 2024).

The established parties are losing ground. There is greater readiness among the public to see far-right agitation as the new normal. Some establishment parties, for instance, mimic AfD demands for a harder line on immigration. But when they do so, support for the AfD actually increases. Right-wing parties have gained much ground in Europe in recent years, but given Germany's past, its success is a disturbingly special case (Fix and Stelzenmüller).

The BfV has been monitoring and investigating the AfD. After it was defined as "a suspected case of right-wing extremism," the party sued the BfV demanding that it rescind the label. The suit was rejected because the office provided ample evidence to support its decision. But the court also took note of the AfD's internal division between moderate and radical wings and of the "formal" dissolution of the latter, concluding that the designation "of more definite extremist aspirations" was not at present warranted (BfV). After four years of investigation, the BfV designated the AfD's chapters in Saxony and Thuringia as cases of extremism and threats to the constitution. It imposed various restrictions on them, particularly on the party's more radical youth organization (Solomon). Thus far, the national party has not been banned.

Public opinion is divided on whether and how the party should be penalized. While many people support a ban, opponents argue that outlawing the party will only increase its support and that AfD supporters would continue to be active in some way or other. They have also demanded that it should be up to the electorate and not the courts to decide how the AfD should be handled (Schuetze, January 21, 2024).

Recently, Chancellor Olaf Scholz alerted the country in a video message: "I will say it clearly and harshly: right-wing extremists are attacking our democracy." Greater public awareness of this this growing threat has led to large-scale protests against the AfD (January 20, 2024). Mobilization by countervailing forces suggests that the party has become more vulnerable.

The United States and Donald Trump

The AfD threatens German democracy, but the threat is far greater in the United States. No mainstream German party has come even close to endorsing the AfD's goals, but in our country, the Republican Party (GOP) has taken a sharp rightward turn. Deep concerns have been widely voiced over the possibility that if former President Trump is reelected, he intends to move the country towards authoritarianism. He plans to retaliate against those who in his view betrayed him, to purge the Department of Justice, appoint only unquestioning loyalists to his cabinet, and weaken the civil service so that he can dismiss officials who have failed to do his bidding. He hopes to invoke a law against insurrection to mobilize the military to crush expected mass opposition. In 2020, Trump sharply criticized Mark Milley, the head of the Joint Chiefs of Staff, when he refused to comply with the president's order to send regular army units to suppress the Black Lives Matter movement. Milley had told him that doing so would violate the longstanding principle of the political neutrality of the armed forces ("If Trump Wins").

If Trump again loses the election 2024, as he did 2020, he will repeat his lie that he lost in 2020 because of widespread electoral fraud and again violate the long-established norm that a defeated candidate must yield to the victor. His contempt for key provisions of the constitution is well known. These threats are real because Trump has prevailed over his rivals in the primary elections to choose the GOP's presidential candidate. His huge popular base has continued to be highly supportive. Millions of Trump supporters agree that the 2020 election was rigged and that Joe Biden is not a legitimate president.

Trump supporters see him as a strongman who can "save our country," echoing Hitler's appeal. The insurrection at the US Capitol on January 6, 2021, staged by armed militias in order to keep the defeated President

Trump in power, resembled the Storm Troopers who set fire to the Reichstag in February 1933, a tactic in the Nazi quest for power. The Nazis blamed communists for this crime; and some far-right American publicists have similarly charged that the assault was actually committed by "anti-fascist" leftist forces (antifa). Trump's supporters trivialize the assault, explaining it away as merely an angry demonstration against electoral fraud.

Resort to violence has become more and more popular. In the 2020 elections, one in six American election workers were threated with violence, some even receiving death threats (Levitsky and Ziblatt, 2023, 123). Alarmingly, a 2021 survey found that 56% of GOP members agreed that "the traditional American way of life is disappearing so fast that we may have to use force to save it" (Ibid, 119). Two years later a survey found that 41% of right-wing citizens and 22% of independents believe that "true American patriots may have to resort to violence to save the country." Only 13% of Democrats shared this view (French). The easy availability of firearms, including military-style automatic weapons, compounds the danger.

The sources of Trump's populist appeal to "Make America Great Again" are similar to those that drive the popularity of the AfD. Angry voters in both countries feel that they have cast aside by the elites who have failed to address their grievances. They are pessimistic about their future, and in this country they believe that they have been deprived of the promises of the "American Dream." These sentiments are common among industrial workers because of widespread offshoring. They are bitter toward companies that invest in China and other countries where labor costs are considerably lower than in the US. As in Germany, voters in deprived rural areas are also severely aggrieved.

Most importantly, Trump's appeal has deep roots in America's turbulent racial history. A cogent explanation is offered in a chapter entitled "Why the Republican Party Abandoned Democracy" in Levitsky and Ziblatt's *The Tyranny of the Minority.* During the civil war Abraham Lincoln's Republican Party fought against slavery and adopted constitutional amendments that guaranteed the civil rights and equal treatment of the emancipated black community. But for a century, during the Jim Crow era, the US largely ignored these commitments and in the southern states African Americans were subjugated by white-imposed laws, practices, and violence.

During the civil rights revolution of the 1960s, the GOP "played a vital role" in the adoption of the Civil Rights and the Voting Rights Acts, thereby supporting the emergence of a more democratic multiracial country (93). But in the decades that followed, the GOP reversed its stance and turned into a predominantly white party dedicated to preserving white privilege. On January 6, 2021, "The full promise and peril of American democracy were on vivid display: a glimpse of a possible multiracial future, followed by an almost unthinkable assault on our constitutional democracy" (Ibid, 4).

This historical transformation came about in response to huge demographic, social, and political changes about which millions of whites are deeply troubled. The non-white population increased substantially after the 1966 liberalization of the immigration law:

> A massive wave of immigration transformed what had been a predominantly white Christian society into a diverse and multiethnic one. . . . Public opinion research shows that for the first time in US history a majority of Americans now embrace ethnic diversity and racial equality—the two key pillars of a multiracial democracy (Ibid, 5–6).

The 1964 and 1965 Civil Rights and Voting Rights Acts sharply increased the visibility and power of minorities. African Americans and Hispanics rose to positions of political, social, cultural, and to some extent economic power. In politics, minority representation in the US Congress and in national, state, and local governments increased significantly. The election of the first Black president in 2012 was a highly visible symbol of this transformation.

Many whites see multiracial democracy as an existential challenge to their identity, primacy, and status. They reacted defensively, as expressed in slogans such as "Take Our Country Back."

As president, and now as the candidate for reelection, Donald Trump gave voice to these feelings. He "signaled to white voters that he intends to maintain the racial hierarchy." He accused a "cabal of elites" of using immigration to replace America's "'native' white population" (Ibid, 117–118). The large-scale crossing of the southern border by illegal migrants, many of whom are non-whites, fueled these fears, which Republicans have turned into a potent political issue.

In 2013, the Supreme Court, with its conservative majority, watered down the Voting Rights Act (VRA), enabling many Republican states to impose voting restrictions to reduce Black voting in a way somewhat reminiscent of the Jim Crow era. This step backwards has made it more difficult for African Americans to vote and run for office in GOP-led states. In 2021, a campaign sought to restore the original VRA. A 2022 survey found that 63%

of voters supported this effort, but a Senate filibuster that required a two-thirds majority thwarted this goal (Ibid, 138).

The rightward turn of US politics has also prompted resurgent antisemitism:

> America's ascendant political movements—MAGA on one side, the illiberal left on the other—would demolish the last pillars of the of the consensus that Jews helped to establish. They regard concepts such as tolerance, fairness, meritocracy, and cosmopolitanism as pernicious shams. . . . Extremist thought and mob behavior have never been good for Jews (Foer).

Neo-Nazis voice the most extreme versions of these sentiments. In 2017, a group of them staged a demonstration in Charlottesville, Virginia, shouting that Jews are "all powerful" but that "they will not replace us." Trump said of this and the ensuing counterdemonstration that there are "fine people on both sides." Chillingly, a photo of an American Nazi shows the man with an SS tattoo: "Meine Ehre heisst Treue" (My Honor means Loyalty). Violent incidents have taken place, exemplified by the 2018 massacre of eleven Jews in a synagogue in Pittsburgh.

The war in Gaza has added another element of political instability in this country. The murderous assault by Hamas on Israeli civilians initially elicited a wide wave of sympathy for Israel. This dissipated because of the Netanyahu government's brutal military campaign, which has destroyed Gaza, caused acute suffering, and killed over thirty thousand civilians. It has fueled an upsurge of international antisemitism and accusations that the government is committing genocide. Outrage is exacerbated by Netanyahu's longstanding determination to thwart Palestinian hopes for an end to the occupation and autonomy or independence for its people. Some far-right members of the cabinet have openly called for ethnic cleansing in Gaza and the West Bank.

A broad coalition of Palestinian Americans and other US students have been protesting vociferously and are severely critical of the Biden administration's unconditional military assistance. They have expressed their deep anger in disruptive demonstrations on many campuses. A good many, however, have not made the essential distinction between the Israeli government and Jews in general, using crude and horrifying language. Such excesses have deeply angered American Jews, including those who support the Palestinian cause (Foer). Inept police efforts to restore calm on campuses have added to the crisis. All this is reminiscent of the massive and sometimes violent movement against the war in Vietnam. Richard Nixon was able to use these events to win the 1968 election. Now, Republicans are again taking advantage of the turmoil in order to boost Trump's reelection campaign.

What can be done to check far-right extremism? America lacks the institutions of Germany's "militant democracy," but our legal system does have laws to bring offenders to account. A large number of the insurrectionists who invaded the US Capitol have been criminally charged, convicted for their actions and sentenced to prison or to payment of heavy fines. For his part, Trump insists that they are patriots and that if he regains the presidency, he will pardon them.

Bringing the former president to account, however, is very problematic. The Fourteenth Amendment, adopted after the civil war, prohibits insurrectionists from holding electoral office. Trump's opponents invoked the Amendment in state courts, but the Supreme Court decided that the issue is a federal one that requires a nationwide verdict. As of writing, it has yet to decide whether Trump should be prevented from running for president. Federal prosecutors in several states have charged him with ninety-one felonies, among them his attempts to reverse President Biden's 2020 victory.

Trump's lawyers claim that he is protected by the First Amendment and enjoys presidential immunity. They have successfully argued for delays in bringing him to trial. The cases are dragging on and may not be resolved even by election day in November. If he is reelected, he could pardon himself. Trump's opponents have criticized the conservative Supreme Court justices for allowing these delays. Its standing as an impartial arbiter has been greatly impaired. The outcome of these forthcoming trials is uncertain. Juries maybe reluctant to convict him.

The criminal charges have angered his supporters and enabled Trump to pose as a victim of judicial persecution, somewhat similar to fears expressed in Germany that inflicting criminal penalties on the AfD would only increase sympathy for the party. Millions accept Trump's claim that he is being framed for political reasons.

Even if found guilty, Trump and his followers will be free to spread lies about established facts and to keep attacking the legitimacy of the electoral system and the judiciary system for its corruption. Millions share these sentiments, which are disseminated on a huge scale by far-right media such as Fox News, the country's most watched news program, as well as by social media. Because of the right-wing media's political bias, the Biden administration's enormous domestic achievements have not had the hoped for impact on public opinion. It feeds the delusions of his devoted followers and further undermines trust in legal and political institutions.

Deeper structural defects have made governance in America increasingly difficult, again calling to mind the economic failures of the Weimar Republic that paved the way for Hitler and the current grievances of the AfD. Our constitution has not kept up with the major demographic and social changes that have taken place since 1789. A striking illustration is the huge imbalance in the size of populations among states. Each state elects two senators for the US Senate, but as of 2022, the two from California represent thirty-nine million people but in Wyoming only 518,000. Senators from the many sparsely populated states thus have disproportionate power to enact or block legislation. Many Americans believe that the constitution must be amended to address these deficiencies, but, given the current polarization, it is virtually impossible to do so.

The country's deep political divisions greatly aggravate the current political paralysis. The "overwhelming majority of electoral districts now lean either to Republicans or Democrats" (Balz and Morse). When one party has a supermajority in a state legislature, primary election contests are decisive and deepen polarization, since fervent partisans tend to vote in them more than those who hold more moderate views. The majority can refuse to compromise with the minority's demands. Much of this situation is due to the gerrymandering of electoral districts, an issue which the Supreme Court has not adequately addressed. These divisions have resulted in "two Americas with competing agendas and values".

Recent surveys show that more and more Americans feel that our institutions are no longer able to deal with urgent policy issues. A large majority believe that issues such as immigration, government deficits, abortion, gun rights, the economy, climate change, and health care are handled "not too well or not at all" by the political process.

How these challenges will play out is an open question. German democracy is under threat, but its political institutions and its relatively progressive economic and social systems suggest that it is well positioned to avoid an authoritarian outcome. In sharp contrast, Americans are confronted by deeply impaired political institutions, by a major decline of social and political trust, which has led to widespread belief that political opponents are enemies and that compromise is therefore not possible. Much time will be needed to find remedies for these deep-seated problems. If this does not happen, millions of people will continue to hope for a strong authoritarian leader who can "save the country."

Photographs

Paul Bernstein, 1930.

Paul at the Habertshof higher boarding school for young workers, with Suzanne Blum, the wife of the school's director.

Johanna Moosdorf with Barbara and Thomas, 1940.

Johanna Moosdorf, 1944.

Barbara, 1950s.

Alice Hanson Cook.

Thomas with his mother in America, 1971.

Johanna Moosdorf, 1996.

Stolperstein (stumbling stone): "Here lived Paul Bernstein, b. 1897, deported to Theresienstadt on January 21, 1944, murdered in Auschwitz, 1944."

Plaque. "The writer Johanna Moosdorf lived in this house from 1959–2000. Born in Leipzig, July 12, 1911; died June 21, 2000, in Berlin. At the heart of her creative work was the necessity that Germany should come to grips with the continuing influence of fascism in daily life. Her depiction of unconventional women is especially noteworthy."

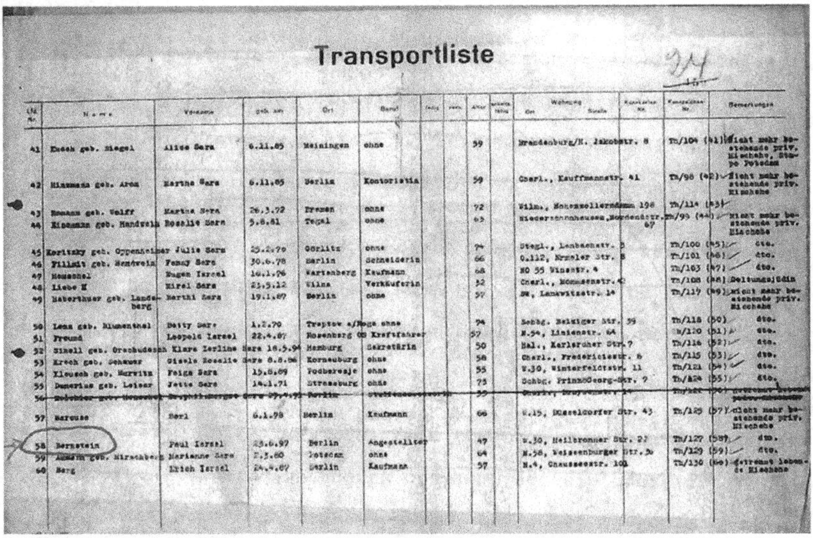

Transportliste

Lfd. Nr.	Name	Vorname	geb. am	Ort	Beruf	[illegible]	[illegible]	Alter	[illegible]	Wohnung Ort Straße	[illegible]	[illegible]	Bemerkungen
41	Kosch geb. Siegel	Alice Sara	6.11.85	Meiningen	ohne			59		Brandenburg/H. Jakobstr. 8		Th/104 (41)	Nicht mehr bestehende priv. Mischehe, Stapo Potsdam
42	Hinzmann geb. Aron	Martha Sara	6.11.85	Berlin	Kontoristin			59		Charl., Kauffmannstr. 41		Th/98 (42)	Nicht mehr bestehende priv. Mischehe
43	Romann geb. Wolff	Martha Sara	26.3.72	Bremen	ohne			72		Wilm., Hohenzollerndamm 198		Th/114 (43)	
44	Eisemann geb. Handwein	Rosalie Sara	5.8.81	Tegel	ohne			63		Niederschönhausen, Nordendstr. 67		Th/99 (44)	Nicht mehr bestehende priv. Mischehe
45	Koritzky geb. Oppenheimer	Julie Sara	25.2.70	Görlitz	ohne			74		Stegl., Lenbachstr. 3		Th/100 (45)	dto.
46	Fillsdt geb. Bernstein	Fanny Sara	30.6.78	Berlin	Schneiderin			66		O.112, Krnsler Str. 8		Th/101 (46)	dto.
47	Menschel	Eugen Israel	16.1.76	Wartenberg	Kaufmann			68		NO 55 Winsstr. 4		Th/103 (47)	dto.
48	Liebe M	Mirel Sara	23.5.12	Wilna	Verkäuferin			32		Charl., Mommsenstr. 42		Th/108 (48)	Geltungsjüdin
49	Haberthuer geb. Landsberg	Berthi Sara	19.1.87	Berlin	ohne			57		SW, Lankwitzstr. 14		Th/117 (49)	Nicht mehr bestehende priv. Mischehe
50	Lena geb. Blumenthal	Betty Sara	1.2.70	Treptow a/Rega	ohne			74		Schbg. Belziger Str. 39		Th/118 (50)	dto.
51	Freund	Leopold Israel	22.4.87	Rosenberg OS	Kraftfahrer			57		N.54, Linienstr. 64		Th/120 (51)	dto.
52	Sinell geb. Orschudesch	Klara Zerline Sara	18.5.94	Hamburg	Sekretärin			50		Hal., Karlsruher Str. 7		Th/116 (52)	dto.
53	Krech geb. Schauer	Gisela Rosalie Sara	8.8.86	Korneuburg	ohne			58		Charl., Fredericiastr. 8		Th/115 (53)	dto.
54	Kleusch geb. Horwitz	Feiga Sara	15.8.89	Podberesje	ohne			55		W.30, Winterfeldtstr. 11		Th/121 (54)	dto.
55	Damerius geb. Leiser	Jette Sara	14.1.71	Strassburg	ohne			73		Schbg. Prinz-Georg-Str. 7		Th/124 (55)	dto.
56	[illegible]	[illegible]	[illegible]	Berlin	[illegible]			59		Charl., [illegible]		[illegible]	[illegible]
57	Marcuse	Beri	6.1.78	Berlin	Kaufmann			66		W.15, Düsseldorfer Str. 43		Th/125 (57)	Nicht mehr bestehende priv. Mischehe
58	Bernstein	Paul Israel	25.6.97	Berlin	Angestellter			47		W.30, Heilbronner Str. 22		Th/127 (58)	dto.
59	Ammann geb. Hirschberg	Marianne Sara	7.3.80	Potsdam	ohne			64		N.58, Weissenburger Str. 30		Th/129 (59)	dto.
60	Berg	Erich Israel	24.4.87	Berlin	Kaufmann			57		N.4, Chausseestr. 101		Th/130 (60)	getrennt lebende Mischehe

Transportliste.

Bibliography

Alternative für Deutschland (AfD). 2016. "Grundsatzprogram für Deutschland" (Basic Program for Germany). May 1, 2016, https://www.afd.de/grundsatzprogramm/.

"Antisemitismus und Rechtsextremismus" (Antisemitism and Rightwing Extremism) Edited by Moses Mendelssohn Zentrum für eurpäisch-jüdische Studies. Potsdam: Center for European-Jewish Studies, October 2023.

Balz, Dan, and Clara Ence Morse. 2023 "American Democracy Is Cracking. These Forces Help Explain Why." *Washington Post,* August 18, 2023. https://www.washingtonpost.com/politics/2023/08/18/american-democracy-political-system-failures/.

Berger, Michael. 2008. "Der Reichsbund Juedischer Frontsoldaten." In *Juedische Soldaten in Deutschen Armeen* (Jewish Soldiers in German Armies), ed. Andreas Kleine-Kraneburg. Berlin: Konrad Adenauer Stiftung.

Brandenburgisches Landeshauptarchiv, Potsdam. Property declarations: Paul Bernstein, Rep. 36A, 3011; Richard, 3006; Regina, 14866.

Bernstein, Paul. 1929. "Die englische Arbeiterbewegung" (The English Workers' Movement). *Arbeiter-Jugend: Monatsschrift der Sozialistischen Arbeiter Jugend Deutschlands* (Monthly Journal for Socialist Young Workers in Germany) 21, no. 5, 110–112.

———. 1929. "Das Internationale Arbeitsamt" (The International Employment Office in Geneva). *Arbeiter-Jugend: Monatsschrift der Sozialistischen Arbeiter Jugend Deutschlands* 21, no. 10, 228–30.

———. 1929. "Oesterreich kann nicht untergehen" (Austria cannot perish). *Arbeiter-Jugend: Monatsschrift der Sozialistischen Arbeiter Jugend Deutschlands* 21, no. 7, 158.

———. 1930. "Die deutschen Parteien nach dem 14. September" (The German Parties after the election in 1930). *Arbeiter-Jugend: Monatsschrift der Sozialistischen Arbeiter Jugend Deutschlands* 22, no. 12, 278–281.

———. 1930. "Die Julirevolution in Frankreich" (The July Revolution in France). *Arbeiter-Jugend: Monatsschrift der Sozialistischen Arbeiter Jugend Deutschlands* 22, no. 7, 158–161.

———. 1930. "Der Nationsozialismus" (National Socialism). *Arbeiter-Jugend: Monatsschrift der Sozialistischen Arbeiter Jugend Deutschlands* 22, no. 6, 129–132.

———. 1931. "Die Diktatur des Reichspraesidenten" (The Special Emergency Powers Given to Presidents by the Weimar Constitution). *Arbeiter-Jugend: Monatsschrift der Sozialistischen Arbeiter Jugend Deutschlands* 23, no. 9, 216.

———. 1931. "Das Ende der britischen Arbeiterregierung" (The End of the British Workers' Government). *Arbeiter-Jugend: Monatsschrift der Sozialistischen Arbeiter Jugend Deutschlands* 23, no. 10, 233–235.

———. 1931. "Das Enzyklika des Pabstes ueber die Ehe" (The Pope's Encyclical on Marriage). *Arbeiter-Jugend: Monatsschrift der Sozialistischen Arbeiter Jugend Deutschlands* 23, no. 5, 118–120.

———. 1931. "Faschismus und Kriegsgefahr" (Fascism and the Danger of War). *Arbeiter-Jugend: Monatsschrift der Sozialistischen Arbeiter Jugend Deutschlands* 23, no. 3, 59–61.

———. 1931. "Die franzoesische Arbeiterbewegung" (The French Workers' Movement). *Arbeiter-Jugend: Monatsschrift der Sozialistischen Arbeiter Jugend Deutschlands* 23, no. 1, 11–14.

———. 1932. "Der Kampf um Preussen" (The Struggle over Prussia). *Arbeiter-Jugend: Monatsschrift der Sozialistischen Arbeiter Jugend Deutschlands* 24, no. 4, 100–104.

———. 1932. "Reaktion ueber Deutschland" (Reaction dominates Germany. *Arbeiter-Jugend: Monatsschrift der Sozialistischen Arbeiter Jugend Deutschlands* 24, no. 9, 263–265.

———. 1932. "Verstaendigung mit Frankreich" (Reaching an Understanding with France). *Arbeiter-Jugend: Monatsschrift der Sozialistischen Arbeiter Jugend Deutschlands* 24, no. 1, 12–15.

———. 1932. "Die Waffen nieder" (Put the Weapons down). *Arbeiter-Jugend: Monatsschrift der Sozialistischen Arbeiter Jugend Deutschlands* 24, no. 2, 38–41.

———1932. "Wandlung der Parteien" (The Transformation of German Parties). *Arbeiter-Jugend: Monatsschrift der Sozialistischen Arbeiter Jugend Deutschlands* 24, no. 6, 168–170.

Bernstein, Eduard. 1907. *Evolutionary Socialism.* London: Independent Labour Party.

BfV. n.d. "Bundesamt für Verfassungsshutz obsiegt vor Verwaltungsgericht Kőln Gegen die Alternative für Deutschland" (The BfV Prevails over the AfD at the Cologne Administrative Court). Accessed April 12, 2024. https://www.verfassungsschutz.de/SharedDocs/pressemitteilungen/DE/2022/pressemitteilung-2022-1-afd.html.

Blum, Emil. 1930. *Der Habertshof: Werden und Gestalt einer Heimvolkshochschule* (Growth and Contour of a Boarding People's Higher School). Kassel: Neuwerk Verlag.

Brandel, Ali. 2023. "Surviving Germany's Neo-Nazi Resurgence." *New Republic,* May 2023, 36–45.

Brezinski, Zbigniew K. 1967. *The Soviet Bloc: Unity and Conflict.* Cambridge, MA Harvard University Press.

Browning, Christopher R. 2017. *Ordinary Men: Reserve Police Battalion 101 and the Final Solution in Poland.* New York: Harper Collins.

Budras, Von Corinna. 2023. "Auf Stimmenfang mit Abstiegsängsten" (Seeking Votes of Those Who Fear Decline). *Frankfurter Allgemeine,* December 30, 2023. https://www.faz.net/aktuell/wirtschaft/mehr-wirtschaft/afd-wirtschaftspolitik-auf-stimmenfang-mit-abstieg-saengsten-19412899.html.

Cook, Alice H. 1990. *A Lifetime of Labor.* New York: Feminist Press at City University of NY.

Czech, Danuta. 1990. *Auschwitz Chronicle, 1939–45: From the Archives of of the Auschwitz Memorial and the German Federal Archives.* New York: Henry Holt and Co.

Dipper, Christof. 1994. "Der 20. Juli und die 'Judenfrage'" (July 20, the Day of the Attempt to Kill Adolf Hitler and the "Jewish Question"). *Die Zeit,* July 8, 1994. https://www.zeit.de/1994/27/der-20-juli-und-die-judenfrage.

"Documenting the Numbers of Victims of the Holocaust and Nazi Persecution." United States Holocaust Memorial Museum. Accessed April 15, 2024. https://www.ushmm.org/search?query=Documenting+the+Numbers+of+Victims+of+the+Holocaust+and+Nazi+Persecution.

Economist. 2023. "Business leaders worry about the rise of the AfD: The last thing the country needs." September 2, 2023. https://www.economist.com/europe/2023/08/31/business-leaders-worry-about-the-rise-of-the-afd.

Entschädigungsamt Berlin. "Wiedergutmachungsakte Paul Bernstein (Restitution Office, Make-Good File, Reg. No. 6309 and 300992, Johanna Moosdorf).

Fest, Joachim C. 1974. *Hitler*. New York: Vintage Books.

Festinger, John. 1995. *Paul Celan: Poet, Survivor, Jew*. New Haven: Yale University Press.

Fix, Liana, and Constanza Stelzenmüller. 2023. "Germany's New Normal? The Surging Far-Right AfD Party Is Upending the Country's Politics." *Foreign Affairs*, October 10, 2023. https://www.foreignaffairs.com/germany/germanys-new-normal.

Foer, Franklin, "The Golden Age of American Jews is ending." *The Atlantic*, March 2024.

Freie Universität Berlin: Zentralinstitut für Sozialwissenschaftliche Forschung. 1995. *Gedenkbuch Berlins: Der jüdischen Opfer des Nationalsozialismus*. Berlin: Freie Universität Berlin. Zentralinstitut für Sozialwissenschaftliche Forschung.

French, David. 2024. "The Greatest Threat Posed by Trump." *New York Times*, January 13, 2024. https://www.nytimes.com/2024/01/12/opinion/donald-trump-culture-decline.html.

Fürst, Michael. 2008. "Juden in Deutschen Armeen—Teil meiner Familiengeschichte. In *Juedische Soldaten in Deutschen Armeen*" (Jews in German Armies—Part of my Family History), edited by Andreas Kleine-Kraneburg, 51–59. Berlin: Konrad Adenauer Stiftung.

Gallagher, Charles R. 2000. "Personal, Private Views: A newly discovered report from 1938 reveals Cardinal Pacelli's anti-Nazi stance." *America*, September 1, 2000. https://www.americamagazine.org/issue/448/article/personal-private-views.

Geheran, Michael. 2020. *Comrades Betrayed: Jewish WWI Veterans under Hitler* (Ithaca: Cornell UP.

"German Jews during the Holocaust, 1939–1945." United States Holocaust Memorial Museum. Accessed April 15, 2024. https://www.ushmm.org/search?query=German+Jews+during+the+Holocaust,+1939–1945.

Grieshaber, Kirsten, 2023. "A win for the far right in Germany." *Los Angeles Times*, July 9, 2023.

Halasz, Martin Schmidt. 2024. "Verfassungsschutzchef erneuert Kritik am AfD: Was motiviert den Chef des BfV?"(He renews critique of AfD: what motivates him?). *Tagesschau* (Daily Show), 7 August, 2023. https://www.tagesschau.de/inland/innenpolitik/haldenwangafd-100.html.

Henry, Frances. 1985/86. "Heroes and Helpers in Nazi Germany: Who Aided Jews?" *Humboldt Journal of Social Relations* 13 (Fall/Winter): 306–319.

Herzig, Arne. 1992. *Verdrängung und Vernichtung der Juden unter dem Nationalsozialismus* (Repression and Extermination of Jews under National Socialism). Hamburg: H. Christians.

Hitler, Adolf. 1935. *Mein Kampf* (*My Struggle*). Muenchen: Zentralverlag der NSDAP.

Horn, Birgit. 1998. *Leipzig im Bombenhagel* (Leipzig during the Hail of Bombs). Leipzig: Schmidt-Roemhild Publishing House.

"If Trump Wins." 2024. *Atlantic*, January/February 2024. https://www.theatlantic.com/if-trump-wins/.

International Military Tribunal. 1948. *Trial of the Major War Criminals before the International Military Tribunal*. Vol. 29. Nuremberg: AMS Press.

Kamman, Matthias. 2017. "Was Höcke mit der 'Denkmal der Schande'-Rede bezweckt" (What Is Behind Höcke's Speech about the "Monument of Shame." *Die Welt*, 18 January, 2017. https://www.welt.de/politik/deutschland/article161286915/Was-Hoecke-mit-der-Denkmal-der-Schande-Rede-bezweckt.html.

Kaplan, Marion A. 1998. *Between Dignity and Despair: Jewish Life in Nazi Germany*. New York: Oxford UP.

Karny, Miroslav, et al. 1995. "Die Theresienstaedter Herbsttransporte" (The Autumn Transports). *Theresienstaedter Studien und Dokumente*: 7–37.

Kavi, Aishvarya, and Christopher F. Schuetze. 2023. "Germany Cracks Down on Another Far-Right Group." New York Times, September 27, 2023. https://www.nytimes.com/2023/09/27/world/europe/germany-far-right-raids.html

Kershaw, Ian. 1998. *Hitler, 1889–1936: Hubris*.

———. 2000. *Hitler, 1935–1945: Nemesis*. New York: W. W. Norton.

Klemperer, Victor. 2015. *Ich will Zeugnis ablegen bis zum letzten: Tagebücher 1933–1945* (I want to bear Witness to the Last: Diaries 1933–1945). 2nd ed. Berlin: Aufbau.

Koop, Volker 2014. *Wer Jude is bestimme ich* (I decide who is a Jew). Cologne: Bohlau Verlag.

Kramer, Stephan J. "Antisemitismus Heute" (Antisemitism Today). In *Juedische Soldaten in Deutschen Armeen*, edited by Andreas Kleine-Kraneburg, 71–76. Berlin: Konrad Adenauer Stiftung.

Krüger, Helmut. 1993. *Der Halbe Stern: Leben als juedischer "Mischling" im Dritten Reich.* (Life as a Half-Jew in the Third Reich). Berlin: Metropol Publisher.

Landesarchiv-Berlin, Paul Bernstein, Rep/026-07, number 860/65.

Lederer, Zdenek. 1983. *Ghetto Theresienstadt*. New York: Howard Fertig.

Levitsky, Steven, and Daniel Ziblatt. 2018. *How Democracies Die*. New York: Penguin Random House.

———. 2023. *Tyranny of the Minority: Why American Democracy Reached the Breaking Point*. New York: Penguin Random House.

Longerich, Peter, ed. 1989. *Die Ermordung der Europäischen Juden: Eine umfassende Dokumentation des Holocaust 1941–45* (The murder of Europe's Jews: A comprehense documentation of the Holocaust). Munich: R. Piper.

———. 1989. "Meldung wichtigerstaatspolitischer Ereignisse des Reichs Sicherheits Hauptamt:Festnahme der Gruppe Baum," May 27, 1942 (Announcement of important-state political occurrences by the Reich Security Main Office: Thearrest of the Baum Group), 405–406. In *Die Ermordung der Europäischen Juden: Eineumfassende Dokumentation des Holocaust* (The murder of Europe's Jews: Acomprehensive documentation), edited by Peter Longerich. Munich: R. Piper.

———. 1989. "Vorbereitung und Organisierung der 'Endlösung' 1941-45"(Preparing and Organizing the 'Final Solution'), 65-73. In *Die Ermordung der Europäischen Juden: Eine umfassende Dokumentation des Holocaust 1941–45* (The murder of Europe's Jews: A comprehense documentation of the Holocaust), edited by Peter Longerich. Munich: R. Piper.

———. 2008. *Heinrich Himmler Biographie*. Munich: Siedler Verlag.

Mai, Karl Detlev und Diehart Krebs. 1986. *Anfangsjahre: Leipzig 1945 bis 1950* (Beginning years). Berlin: DirkNischen.

Ministry of Propaganda of the Third Reich. 1944. The *Führer Gives a City to the Jews* (*Der Führer schenkt den Juden eine Stadt*). Waltham, MA: The National Center for Jewish Film, 1991. DVD.

Monroe,Kristen R. 1998. *The Art of Altruism:Perceptions of a Common Community*. Princeton: Princeton University Press.

Moosdorf, Johanna. 1964. *Nebenan* (*Next Door*). New York: Alfred. A. Knopf. 1947.

———. *Brennendes Leben* (Burning Life). Berlin: JHW Dietz, 1947.

———. 1989. *Jahrhunderttraume* (Dreams of the Century). Frankfurt: Fischer Taschenbuch Verlag.

———.1992. *Die Andermanns*. 2nd. ed. Frankfurt: Fischer Taschenbuch Verlage.

Noakes, Jeremy. 1989. "The Development of Nazi Policy towards the German-Jewish 'Mischlinge,' 1933–1945." *Leo Baeck Institute Yearbook* 34 (1).

Ozment, Steven. 2004. *A Mighty Fortress: A New History of the German People*. New York: Harper-Collins.

Parks, Tim. 2022. "The Pope's Many Silences." *New York Review of Books*, October 20, 2022.

Pasher, Yaron. 2014. *Holocaust vs. Wehrmacht: How Hitler's "Final Solution" Undermined the German War Effort*. Lawrence: University Press of Kansas.

Poll, Robert. 2024. "The Weimar Constitution: Germany's First Democratic Constitution, Its Collapse, and the Lessons for Today." kas.de., May 2020. https://www.kas.de/documents/265308/265357/The+Weimar+Constitution.pdf/a6021d8d-82d2-47cf-7e37-0a314be02d9e?version=1.1&t=1590565540705.

Richter, Christoph. 2023. "'Wer wählt rechtsaußen?' Strukturelle Erfolgsbedingungen der AfD bei Bundes- und Landtagswahlen in Brandenburg" ("Who votes for the far right?"). Moses Mendelssohn Zentrum für europäisch-jüdische Studien. https://www.mmz-potsdam.de/forschung/emil-julius-gumbel-forschungsstelle/mitteilungen/wer-waehlt-rechtsaussen-strukturelle-erfolgsbedingungen-der-afd.

Schuetze, Christopher F. 2024. "Germans Push Back as Far Right's Influence Grows." *New York Times*, January 20, 2024. https://www.nytimes.com/2024/01/20/world/europe/far-right-germany-fear.html.

———. "Protests against the German Far Right Gain New Urgency as Party Ascends" *New York Times*, January 21, 2024. https://www.nytimes.com/2024/01/20/world/europe/far-right-germany-fear.html.

Sifton, Elizabeth, and Fritz Stern. 2022. "The Tragedy of Dietrich Bonhoeffer and Hans von Dohnanyi." *New York Review of Books*, October 20, 2022.

Solomon, Erika, 2023. "Germany Deems Youth Wing of Far-Right Party an Extremist Group." *New York Times*, April 26, 2023. https://www.nytimes.com/2023/04/26/world/europe/germany-afd-youth-wing-extremist.html.

Steinecke, Gerhard. 2005. *Drei Tage im April: Kriegsende in Leipzig* (Three Days in April: The End of the War in Leipzig). Leipzig: Lehmsted Verlag.

Stern, Fritz. 2006. *Five Germany's I have Known*. New York: Farrar, Straus, and Giroux.

Stoppard, Tom. 2020. *Leopoldstadt*. New York: Grove Press.

"The Treatment of Soviet POWs: Starvation, Disease, and Shootings, June 1941–January 1942." United States Holocaust Memorial Museum. Accessed April 15. https://www.ushmm.org/search?query=treatment+of+Soviet+POWs:+Starvation,+Disease.

"Transportliste" (http://www.statistik-des-Holocaust.de/TT100-3.jpg).

Venske, Regula. 1987. "Schriftstellerin gegen das Vergessen: Johanna Moosdorf" (Writer against Forgetting: Johanna Moosdorf). In *Frauenliteratur ohne Tradition: Neun Autorinnenportraits* (Women's Literature without Tradition: Nine Portraits), edited by Inge Stephan et al, 191–220. Frankfurt: Fischer Taschenbuch Verlag.

———. 1993. "'. . . uns bringen sie vielleicht um, aber du mußt weiterleben mit denen . . .' —Johanna Moosdorf" ('. . . perhaps they will kill us, but you must go on living with them . . .'). In *Zwischen Aufbruch und Verfolgung* (Between New Beginnings and Persecution), edited by Denny Hirschbach and Sonia Nowoselski. Winterthur: Zeichen und Spuren Verlag.

———. 2001, "Hubert Schönung: Als Fremdling an ihrem Sarg: EineLeichenrede" (As a stranger at her coffin: A funeral oration), 177-183. In *WarumLeben: Eine Lesebuch mit Original Texte* (Why live: A reader withoriginal texts), edited by Regula Venske. Bern: Scherz.

Wannsee-Konferenz vom 20. Januar 1942: Analyse und Dokumentation, ed. Peter Klein. Berlin: Edition Hentrich, n.d).

Weber, Thomas. 2010. *Hitler's First War*. New York: Oxford University Press.

Wikipedia. 2024. S.v." 1930 German Federal Election data." Last modified March 17, 2024. https://en.wikipedia.org/wiki/1930_German_federal_election.

Wikipedia. 2004. S.v. "Bernhard Lichtenberg." Last modified March 22, 2024. https://en.wikipedia.org/wiki/Bernhard_Lichtenberg.

Wikipedia, 2024. S.v. "Herbert Baum." Last modified on March 22, 2004. https://en.wikipedia.org/wiki/Herbert_Baum.

Wikipedia. 2024. S.v. "March 1933 German federal election." Last modified March 17, 2024. https://en.wikipedia.org/wiki/March_1933_German_federal_election.

Wikipedia. 2024. S.v. "*Frontkämpferprivileg*" (Privilege for frontline soldiers). 2020g. Last modified March 1, 2024. https://en.wikipedia.org/wiki/Frontk%C3%A4mpferprivileg.

Wikipedia. 2024. S.v. "Globke, Hans." Last modified, April 11, 2024. https://wikipedia.org/wiki/Hans_Globke.

Wikipedia. 2024. S.v. "Kniefall von Warschau." Last modified April 9, 2024. https://en.wikipedia.org/wiki/Kniefall_von_Warschau.

Wikipedia. 2024. S.v. "Weimar paramilitary groups." Last modified March 22, 2024. https://en.wikipedia.org/wiki/Weimar_paramilitary_groups.

"Willy Brandt—Stations in his political life." n.d. Willie Brandt: Online Biografie. Accessed April 12, 2024. https://www.willy-brandt-biography.com.

Wilsack, Connie, Jonathan Webber, and Teresa Świebocka, eds. 1993. *Auschwitz: A History in Photographs*. Bloomington: Indiana University Press.

Wir Waren Nachbarn—Biographien jüdischer Zeitzeugen (We Were Neighbors—Biographies of Jewish Witnesses). Rathaus Schöneberg, Berlin, 2005. Exhibition.

Index

www.ingramcontent.com/pod-product-compliance
Lightning Source LLC
Jackson TN
JSHW011739040225
78443JS00004B/254

* 9 7 9 8 8 8 7 1 9 6 1 9 0 *